Direct

The Personnel Job of
Government Managers

The Personnel Job of Government Managers

O. GLENN STAHL

INTERNATIONAL PERSONNEL MANAGEMENT ASSOCIATION

1313 EAST 60th STREET, CHICAGO, ILLINOIS 60637

Foreword

THIS BOOK is addressed primarily to the government manager. The author, Dr. O. Glenn Stahl, has performed a genuine service to public administration by clearly defining the role of managers and supervisors in personnel matters. So far as we know this book is the only contemporary text written expressly for program directors and supervisors in government operations.

The heart of *The Personnel Job of Government Managers* is an analysis of how program managers can and should participate and become involved in the major personnel functions. In this delineation the author neatly combines theory and practice. He treats the major tenets of personnel management and at the same time gives many practical, down-to-earth suggestions about how the program manager and supervisor can put those tenets to work. Without resort to corny cliches, Dr. Stahl shows how the program manager can speed personal growth and development of associates and subordinates to obtain both productivity and satisfaction.

v

Readers will find this book brief, direct, and to the point. It gives a balanced view, but it does not mince words. It is succinct, but packed with ideas and helpful thinking. It is a zesty, fresh approach to old and persistent issues. It is so written that it may be read in one sitting, or it may serve as a tool in training programs.

The book is equally applicable to all levels of public service in the United States and Canada—federal, state or provincial, county, and municipal. It is suitable for international agencies and governments in many other countries. In fact, many private corporations here and abroad will find the book useful in building managerial competence into their staffs.

While addressed primarily to managers, this little volume can profitably be read by personnel officials themselves. They can gain insights that will help them clarify their own thinking about how the personnel man can and should serve management.

In this book, Dr. Stahl distills the knowledge gained during many years of distinguished public service. When he retired in 1969 as Chief, Bureau of Policies and Standards, U.S. Civil Service Commission, he had spent nearly 34 years in the federal service. In addition to distinguished service in a variety of governmental agencies, Dr. Stahl has served as consultant to a number of governments overseas, including Venezuela, Nepal, and India. He is the author of the basic college-level text, *Public Personnel Administration* (Harper and Row, 6th Edition, 1971) and of many articles and other publications. He has served as adjunct professor of public administration at The American University and as visiting lecturer at other universities. Dr. Stahl is the recipient of many honors and awards, including the U. S. Civil Service Commission's Award for Distinguished Service, the Society for Personnel Administration's Stockberger Award, and the National Civil

Service League's Career Service Award. He is an Honorary Lifetime Member of the Public Personnel Association, and has served the Association as Executive Council member and as President. For these reasons, we are especially proud to have the opportunity to present what we feel is a very significant contribution to the literature of public administration.

KENNETH O. WARNER

Preface

T HE INTENDED AUDIENCE for this book may be
anywhere in the managerial family: the "big brass" in
the front office, middle-management, or supervisors down
the line. They may have come up through the ranks or from
private employment as specialists—engineers, doctors, lawyers, economists, accountants, social workers, tax collectors,
scientists, or practitioners in other fields of expertise.
Whatever their origin, they now are managers with responsibility for getting the public's work done through
groups of employees, they now are concerned with "personnel."

This is not a handbook or reference tool in which
one can simply look up the answers to problems. It is a
"backgrounder", a bit of insight and counsel to equip
public executives mentally and emotionally for the trying
tasks of hiring, deploying, assigning, supervising, disci-
plining, and—above all—inspiring employees to work their
hearts out for the public interest.

The volume is neither a demonstration of how to

hoodwink employees nor an apologia on how to keep them happy. It is a straightforward statement of the responsibilities of public managers in the field of personnel administration, an area which parallels their responsibilities for other aspects of their jobs. If the reader is looking for ways around the system, he should close this book right now. For this presentation is hard-nosed, realistic advice on what government managers need to know, what they have to do, what being a public official is all about—not a primer on how to make the job easier. The job is tough. This little volume simply helps prepare one for facing up to that fact of life.

The underlying thesis is that the public executive is as responsible for developing and implementing personnel policies as are the personnel specialists—more so, in fact; for the main grist of personnel work is in the day-to-day assignment of duties, in teaching and leading staff members, and in holding workers to high standards of performance. The operating manager of a public office, the supervising engineer on a highway project, the doctor in charge of a hospital or clinic, the lawyer supervising the preparation of a set of regulations, the accountant directing a staff of computer technicians and financial experts— are all personnel directors in the truest sense of the word. And, they are accountable for how well the personnel job is done.

The purpose of this book is to explore how public personnel policies became what they are; how some require improvement (a condition which can be corrected by knowledgeable executives); and how executives can meet their own goals more satisfactorily and at the same time serve public policy objectives better in the arena where personnel management is mainly practiced—in the daily assignment and supervision of people.

A more detailed discussion of the personnel function

and its place in public administration—designed especially for the personnel practitioner, for those who develop personnel policy, and for students of the subject in the United States and abroad—will be found in the author's *Public Personnel Administration,* Sixth Edition (Harper & Row, Publishers, New York: 1971).

A highly selective bibliography is included at the end of this book. Any point that a reader finds treated too briefly in this purposely thin volume is covered more completely in some one or several of the works listed.

O. GLENN STAHL.

Contents

1

The Demands on
Government Administration

THE MORE technical and affluent a society becomes,
the more complex and unrelenting are its problems.
Many institutions work at solving those problems or keeping them within some tolerable bounds, but only one institution deals with all of them—an institution that is the
property of all of us—namely, government.

Within the framework of government—federal, state,
local, and even international—the part that renders the
services, makes the regulations, handles the cases, answers the questions, issues the permits, and runs the
institutions is the machinery of administration. Important
as are the policy-making and overseeing functions of the
legislative bodies, and the interpretative and arbitrative
functions of the judiciary, nothing quite matches the
phenomenal size and daily impact of the administrative
organs of government.

Sometimes referred to disparagingly as the "bureaucracy" (although the term is not intrinsically invidious

and is equally applicable to all large organizations, public or private), the administrative machinery of the modern state is indeed a most remarkable and intricate set of man-made enterprises. In the United States, public administration—from running public schools and building public roads, to operations involved in national defense and international representation—employs one-sixth of the working population. It also acts as steward for a major portion of the country's real estate and other wealth, exerts the most profound influence on the national income and growth, and to a considerable degree determines the rules of the game for the private sector. The civil services making up this giant administrative complex are engaged in every occupation known to man. They have become so extensive and difficult to comprehend as to create ever-changing problems of direction and control. Their characteristics, the obligations and privileges of their members, their forms of organization are the objects of never-ending scrutiny and inquiry, not only by the other organs of government but also by scholars and private associations of many varieties.

Those members of civil services who occupy positions of top-level supervision and management, hereafter referred to as *government managers,* are usually quite aware of the immensity and involved character of their tasks. Sometimes they feel inadequately prepared to face them. Often no amount of education, experience, or human ingenuity seems to be equal to the challenge; but this, of course, is what keeps it interesting. Public executives have the most trying of responsibilities, but they also have some of the most fascinating and intriguing ones.

Since government administration is no better than its system for attracting, rewarding, and motivating its civil servants, one of the most challenging responsibilities of government managers is in the area of personnel administration. The task is not just a side issue, a chore to be put up with; nor is it simply the function of those spending full time on personnel policy and operation. The thesis of this book is that the personnel function is absolutely central to the accomplishment of work, to serving the mission of the public agency; and that it is a principal component of every government manager's job. To see this point in full perspective is the purpose of this chapter.

Size, Complexity, and Responsiveness

The imperishability of government of, by, and for the people depends on the accountability and responsiveness of the public bureaucracy. The citizen who finds government agencies confusing and bewildering at best, or insolent and careless at worst, hardly feels like a citizen of a democracy. The taxpayer who detects favoritism in the face of organized pressure, who feels that "the little man" has no power, who is unable to get a rational explanation for action or lack of action which hurts him—is a poor prospect for returning a square deal to his government. The very size, complexity, and impersonality of modern government—inevitable though it is, considering the vast array of public problems that must be dealt with—make accountability to the public and sensitivity to human needs all the more difficult to attain.

Most government managers are mindful of the necessity to lean over backwards to maintain a "service" attitude. They appreciate that in this all-too-mechanized world they are not owners of authority but agents of public purpose. They understand why representatives of the people must be listened to, why public employees must be inspired with a sense of mission, why the gauge of their success is the ability to carry out public policy in the spirit, not just the letter, of the law. At the same time they sense their obligation to consider all sides, to think about the interests of those not immediately pressing their cases as well as of those who are, and to insure the utmost impartiality of their staffs. In short, everywhere they turn they must face up to issues relating to the quality and behavior of the civil servants working for and with them.

The simple fact is this: the responsiveness of our vast public administrative machine, its willingness to be held accountable for what it does—indeed the viability of organized democracy itself—are vitally dependent on the selection, training, and motivation of our public servants, from executives on down to those who deal across the counter with the average citizen. Mere ability and knowledge is not enough. Execution of the laws demands the utmost in ethical behavior, social awareness, capacity to sense the needs of others, adaptability to change, and ability to relate one's own functions in proper perspective to others; it also means being interested enough to know where in the governmental maze some need can be met, and to facilitate its getting done. So much depends on attitude, and the attitude of the people in a bureaucracy depends on the leadership of government managers.

Policy and Administration

Contrary to the shibboleth to which some still give credibility, public administration is not confined to carrying-out roles only; the sheer magnitude and technical character of serving public needs give administrators major policy roles as well. The public servant who denies this is practicing a form of self-delusion or outright dishonesty.

Much, if not most, of the work of modern legislative bodies originates in the bowels of the bureaucracy. Experts even at second and third echelons are often involved in shaping and influencing prospective legislation. Even taking into account the impact of outside groups pressing their viewpoints upon legislative committees, the power of the bureaucrat in developing new laws and amending old ones is scarcely exceeded by any other party to the process. Also, in the execution of laws, the details must be left to administrative agencies. The regulations that fill in the interstices among broad expressions of objective in legislation are the work of public servants. Their zeal for the public welfare, their integrity, and their faithfulness to the statutory aims must be balanced with their predilections and personal viewpoints.

Indeed, administration is policy almost as much as it is application. Granted that the leadership in developing new programs and laws falls to the politically elected heads, such officials are making increased use of the expertise and initiative of the career men and women in the upper strata of the permanent bureaucracy. The career people involved are the government managers—with whom we are here largely concerned—and their immediate subordinates. One of the special demands upon these career managers is to see that the policy sensitivity of the staff is as carefully nurtured as its expert knowledge.

Requisites for Executive Performance

And there is more to our expectations of the modern government executive. In fact, merely defining what to-day's public service manager must be like is to seem to describe a paragon of intelligence, virtue, and adaptability. At least four requisites stand out.

Breadth of View

First, the government manager must develop perspective beyond his special field. He must overcome the myopia of his specialization and see its relationships to other government activities and to the private arena. He must not, as the great British scholar and statesman Harold J. Laski put it, "sacrifice the insight of common sense to intensity of experience." He must develop the ability to accept new views in spite of his preoccupation with his own conclusions. He must see all sides of and around his subject. Laski feared that the expert was too likely to "make his subject the measure of life, instead of making life the measure of his subject," to mistake "technical results for social wisdom."

In other terms, the public executive has to be a judge, not merely an advocate. His responsibility is not to press the interests of his special province so much as to determine where it fits into a larger whole. When issues of budget and time priorities emerge, his obligation is not merely to defend his own function; he must also assess and interpret where it stands in the overall scheme, clarifying its rational place in the totality of public purpose.

Ability to Grow

Second, the government manager has an obligation to grow. Standing pat is seldom a virtue—except on the most fundamental of principles. Neither the tenets of specialization nor the criteria of yesterday belong in this fundamental category. To use John W. Gardner's term, the crowning need for the modern executive is for periodic *self-renewal.* Whether this renewal is done by wide reading, formal training, sheer will power, or all three, it is an imperative of the modern public administrator. Re-examining one's assumptions, to say nothing of one's information, is a necessity in a world of change. For those in leadership positions in government—which should be monitoring change—it is a compelling necessity.

Agent of Change

Third, and closely related, the executive must be personally receptive to change. Instead of viewing his role as that of maintaining the status quo, the government manager must think of himself as being in charge of change. He cannot afford simply to respond, he must initiate; in fact, he must innovate. The image of the modern public executive is a dynamic one—on the move, charting new courses, blazing new trails—not merely protecting the methods and objectives of yesteryear.

Concern for People

Finally, the government manager must have a genuine concern for people. Whatever his field, however mechanical or non-social, the supervisor who has no time for the sticky problems of human relationships, who views them as encroachments on his time and patience, will not be successful either as a supervisor or as a true servant of the people. The point is that an interest in and regard for human beings and their problems is as much a part of the public executive's operating responsibilities as it is of his role as a supervisor. His responsibilities extend to having an implicit faith in people, a confidence that the best is to be expected of them until proved otherwise.

A Contributing Instrument for Action

The government manager who seeks to exemplify these qualities—perspective, self-renewal, adaptability to change, and people-mindedness—will find that one of the channels through which he can develop such attributes is in personnel administration. It is in personnel administration that he will find, in microcosm, some representation of the general public. In the direction and motivation of his staff he develops the skills of garnering the contributions of others, testing the efficacy of ideas, resolving varying points of view without creating bitterness, persuading people to collaborate together, facing the unpleasant as well as the satisfying, and inspiring enthusiastic adherence to lofty purposes. In short, not only is the personnel function an inescapable and important aspect of every public managerial job, it is a positive asset in serving the operating aims of every public function.

The thesis is as simple as this: every governmental activity exists because it is a service to the people; such service is performed by a special corps of workers, civil servants; the government manager's responsibility is met by effective, direct use of that corps and by recognizing that such use is an internal proving ground for his obligations to the public at large. This is the essence of the personnel function. It is not only a way of life within the enterprise, it is the organization's main link with its environment.

To say this calls for some elaboration at this point concerning what the personnel function is all about—and also what it is not.

2

What the Personnel
Function Is All About

SOME OF THE mysteries of personnel policy and operation may seem strange indeed to the uninitiated specialist who suddenly finds himself elevated to a leadership post in the public service. Perhaps he has had some experience as an employee, either in the particular jurisdiction or elsewhere, and has heard many statements about the personnel function, some correct, others pure myth. Except as some event or development affected his own status or prospects, he may have given the subject scarcely a second thought.

He is often the prisoner of those fellow workers who complain about the deficiencies in personnel activities, especially colleagues who have been disappointed in their own careers and look for some scapegoat on which to place the blame. Occasionally, he hears of new objectives or new nomenclature such as: manpower planning, motivation, human relations, collective bargaining, management by purpose, the supervisor as trainer, and a host of other—

sometimes poorly defined—concepts or techniques. He may even have been exposed to some formal training, through conferences and seminars, in the arts of supervision and other presumed subtleties of the personnel process.

The Question of Merit

More often than not he has accepted the fact that his city, state, federal, or other public agency handles its personnel operations under a plan described as a "merit system". Of course, he may work in one of the few localities where there is no pretense of merit being the governing factor and where he knows perfectly well that methods for selection, reward, and advancement are indefensible on any rational, moral, or practical grounds. If this should be the case, much of what is set forth here will seem far removed from the realities of his experience.

However, if the budding executive works in one of the major cities, in one of the larger or more progressive states (or certain fields of service in any state), in the United States federal government (with few exceptions), or in any number of international bodies, he will almost certainly be expected to operate within a going-concern framework that professes to live by the ideal of merit as the guiding principle in recruiting, evaluating, promoting, and retaining public personnel. The merit system—sometimes mistakenly called "civil service"—now predominates in the American public service and in most of the major nations of the world.

Almost all large American cities and about two-thirds of the states have service-wide merit systems. Medium-size municipalities have at least large segments of their administrative operations under merit procedures. With reference to certain functions which are financed in part or entirely by federal funds (such as public welfare, health, employment services, unemployment insurance, and vocational rehabilitation) the states must follow federal employment policies which are based on merit. While few counties have formal merit systems, those that do play important roles in several metropolitan areas.

The Merit Idea in Public Employment

Curious notions still persist about what a merit system is supposed to be, to say nothing about what it actually is. Some people equate it with written tests; others are obsessed with the idea that a "civil service" employee has lifetime tenure and cannot be separated—come what may. Less extreme distortions also prevail. For example, some people innocently assume that the particular procedural features of some system with which they are familiar—such as eligibility limited to local residents, periodic examinations with set date limits, a grade of seventy as a passing point in tests, selection by administrative officials from among the top three candidates, and the like—are necessary absolutes in any merit system. Such mistaken notions are so widespread that it is imperative that a few fundamentals be stressed—what the merit idea means, what it does not mean, and how it got that way.

A Definition

Essentially the merit idea is a statement of objective, not a procedure. A wide variety of procedures may comport with the basic concept. Merit initially was applied solely to the manner of entrance into the service; now the concept is used to convey a much broader spectrum of personnel policies and practices. The nub of the merit idea is that *a person's worth to the organization—the merit of his attributes and capacities—is the governing factor in his*

11

selection, assignment, pay, recognition, advancement, and retention. Other considerations—such as sex, race, religion, political affiliation, economic status, age, and so forth—are irrelevant and have no proper place in implementing the merit objective.

Many aspects of personnel administration may not seem to fit into this definition; but the merit idea is fundamental even with reference to such distantly-related issues as training, unionism, ethics, motivation, and communication. As an objective, the merit system is a key to all parts of the personnel function; it is entirely appropriate, therefore, to think of it as connoting the totality of a public personnel system.

How It Came About

The common-sense character of the merit objective seems so natural to most Americans that many people wonder why it should ever have been inoperative. After all, the American economic system, the most phenomenal the world has ever known, is founded on a rugged selective process which emphasizes personal qualities of capacity, industriousness, and productivity. The criteria may not always have been appropriate; competition has not always been fair; but competition there was, and the responsibilities and the rewards—with countless, exceptions of course—have gone to those who could measure up in terms of intelligence, knowledge, and perseverence. This has been true not only in the economic arena, in the money-making process, but also in achievement in the professions and other walks of life. Ours has clearly been an achieving society; and, in spite of our reverence for individualism, it has been built on the collective and collaborative efforts of groups—partnerships, corporations, schools, unions, and other institutions.

The history of achievement and merit in government

employment is not so readily explained. Here the factors and forces were more complex. In the early days of the republic competence was taken for granted. The founders of the new state and federal governments made up an aristocracy of competence. However, as the pressures of a frontier and grass-roots democracy built up, resentment against the concentration of competence and rewards in traditional, educated sectors of American society became heated.

Democracy and the Spoils. Little wonder that new principles of government employment came to be espoused in the time of Andrew Jackson and for half a century thereafter. These principles held that the "little man"—the farmer, the shopkeeper, the laborer—deserved representation in government service; that most public jobs could be readily learned by any reasonably bright, well-meaning person; and that the best way to open opportunities in the service for all strata of the populace was to fill public jobs with the supporters of those who won elective office. And so we came upon the phrase, "to the victor belong the spoils." Thus, the scheme of job patronage under which political party loyalty and service were the supreme tests for acquiring government jobs, from the lowest to the highest, came to be known as the "spoils system."

Some students of the subject make a good case for such a system in its time. All but a few government jobs were non-technical and required little formal preparation. Moreover, service to the party was a kind of competition that winnowed out those who did not have the interest, motivation, or stamina to deserve attention and reward by political leaders.

But government did not remain non-technical very long. Throughout the nineteenth century, developing public education, building public roads, collecting taxes, regulating business enterprise, monitoring public health, and a host of other insistent tasks began to call for new

13

kinds of competence, rather remote from that generated by the grubby experience in the wards and precincts in political campaigns.

Furthermore, patronage and the spoils process had sowed the seeds of their own corruption. The politicians really had no systematic way of determining who among their followers were most deserving of the plums of political fortune. It was a pretty hit-or-miss affair. Also, as the economy expanded, enterprising men and women were attracted to business and the professions; and those who were totally dependent on job hand-outs in government service tended to be the lazy, the misfits, and the ne'er-do-wells.

In a comparatively short span of years, between the 1840s and the 1880s, the spoils system became entrenched in every state and city and even much of the federal government. It had come to be associated with relative incompetence and obsequious fawning of public employees on their political sponsors in order to stay in their good graces. Moreover, the turnover of employees every time political leadership changed had reached the point of intolerability.

The Need For Change. By mid-century wise and public-spirited men had begun to argue for change. They could see the debilitating effects on government operations —the listless attitudes, lack of productivity, outright corruption. It became increasingly evident that many public workers were little more than the sycophants of their political sponsors; they felt no loyalty or obligation to the public as a whole and were easy pawns in acts of favoritism and shady dealings when their sponsors demanded such performance. There was no incentive anywhere in the set-up for competent, impartial, honest administration. Public jobs were merely political currency; and public employees were, for the most part, merely products that could be bought with that currency. Often they were required to "kick back" part of their pay to party treasuries. This total situation was the shame of our cities and the degradation of our states.

This is not the place to elaborate on the full history of the reform and change that began to take place in the 1880s and on up to the 1930s. The groundwork had been laid by the great reformers, and the turning point was the assassination of President Garfield by a disappointed office seeker. The changes took the form of new laws pertaining to the civil service—hence the phrase that stuck, "civil service laws." The first steps were taken by the federal government, followed almost immediately by action in several of the states.

The new laws sought to replace the spoils system with a merit system. Although halting and limited in initial application, most of them provided for future extension. One jurisdiction after another fell into line in the decades that followed. In fact, new conquests for the merit idea were still being made in the 1960s.

The Ingredients of Merit

The impetus for the merit concept was an ethical one in the broadest political sense. Sound government, competent government, fair government were impossible without it. Indeed, the very foundations of the democratic philosophy were at stake. Curiously, what had started out as a device to insure opportunities for the masses in government employment—job patronage—had degenerated into a liability for them. Only the dregs of society gained from the system and they were not gaining very much. Their incompetence as government payrollers served to keep salaries at pitifully low levels; and they, like the rest of the public, suffered from the ill effects of poor public services.

The main ingredient of the merit idea, therefore, was to break out of this wasteful and harmful syndrome by

15

providing a completely different basis for determining who shall get government employment. It was an ingredient designed to insure both competence and open opportunity. It sought both excellence and fairness. It was, in short, *competition*—competition on the basis of the relative qualifications of candidates for the work to be performed.

Over the years, the enduring elements of competition for public jobs have been:

1. Adequate publicity about government job openings —so that they are not available only to those with "inside" information, and so that all interested citizens can learn about the opportunities.
2. Genuine opportunity for interested citizens to apply —so that they have a chance to make their interest known and to receive consideration.
3. Realistic and fairly-applied standards—so that the qualifications required for eligibility are reasonably related to the occupation and are applied impartially and equally to all who make their interest known.
4. Absence of inappropriate discrimination—so that factors other than those reflecting ability and fitness for employment do not enter into the standards.
5. Ranking on the basis of qualifications—so that the selection process gives effect to evaluations of the relative ability and fitness of candidates.
6. Knowledge of results—so that the public is aware of how the process works; and so that anyone believing that it has not been properly applied in his case has a chance for administrative review.

In the face of the conditions that were being corrected, it should be clear why each of these elements of competition was considered vital to a true merit system. A thoughtful reading of these points will go far to explain some of what seems to be the abracadabra of existing merit processes: waiting time before examinations are given, ranking of candidates in some formal order of relative merit, insistence that appointments be only on the basis of that ranking, restrictions on temporary "out-of-order" appointments, and so on.

Some Encrustations and Problems

Adaptability. The effort over the years to reconcile these imperatives of merit and competition with burgeoning demands of new occupations and critical urgencies throughout the public service has created frequent stresses and strains. Some jurisdictions have become so enamored with particular *methods* that had long ago been established to implement these *principles* of competition that they have lost sight of the original intent; they have failed to see that alternate methods, more suitable to modern needs, could serve the twin objectives of quality and fairness just as well.

For example, the old practices of having closing dates on all examinations and separate competitions for each job or occupation has generally given way to the "open, continuous examination," under which applicants can enter the competition at any time and be eligible for a broad spectrum of related jobs. Also, new techniques of gauging general abilities have commonly replaced examinations for specific knowledges or skills. Any jurisdiction that does not make use of such devices is most certainly behind the times.

Credentialism. More invidious has been the manner in which minimum standards for entry have been arrived at. Too often personnel agencies have accepted without question criteria laid down by the organized members of professions and other occupations. Many such groups have been striving to keep their standards high but also have kept entrance to the field limited. Thus, rigid educational or other requisites have been prescribed as a *sine qua non* for many fields of endeavor without reference to the precise skills and knowledges necessary to perform the work. In other words, such standards, instead of being arrived at by careful job analysis, have been dictated by arm-chair cerebration of the high moguls of the occupational hierarchy.

The sins of the personnel people lie not in their having created such requirements but in having accepted them too uncritically. Ours is a credential-ridden society; the credentials necessary to break into almost all highly-skilled fields, especially the professions (and those occupations that aspire to be professions), have in many cases been unrealistic, unreasonable, or both. Witness also the long-standing four-year apprenticeships required for entrance into some of the oldest skilled trades. Although many of these standards have brought solid improvement in the quality of the practitioners, they have also insured their scarcity. Thus, when a supervisor complains about the artificiality or rigidity of requirements set for entry into his occupation, he had better look to the leadership of his own group as the place to start reform. He should expect his personnel officials to cooperate in or even initiate such an endeavor, but they can seldom risk a change without some support from the occupation's high priesthood.

Some Omissions. There are other shortcomings to the interpretation of merit as it has been practiced in American public services. Too much emphasis has been placed on raw intellectual or technical capacity with too little cognizance of such qualities as creativity, courage, and commitment. More will be said about this deficiency later. The point made here is simply to record that there is more to merit than what some examinations measure. Unfortunately some guardians of the merit principle have mistakenly looked on certain qualities of great importance to successful performance as extraneous, or as adequately taken care of by the latitude left to appointing officials in choosing from among the top candidates. For example, requiring that successful candidates evidence real sympathy, even zeal, for the public program on which they seek to work is not only compatible with, but often essential to, the attainment of true merit.

Myths About Testing. Although further details can be left to a later chapter, another problem lies in the issue of written tests. As indicated earlier, some superficial observers assume that competitive merit determinations require written tests; they thereupon ascribe all flaws in testing to the basic merit principle. The mistake is in the initial premise. Written tests serve very useful purposes, but they are by no means the backbone of competition itself.

Quite valid methods for distinguishing among candidates are also to be found in systematic comparison of the nature, level, quality, and progression of experience relevant to the field of work. Intensive investigation into candidates' previous performance lends itself to objective analysis and comparison when the time and trouble are taken to do it well. Oral testing has been developed into a respectable measuring instrument when carefully and properly applied. Various combinations of these and other evaluative methods are used successfully by many progressive jurisdictions.

While it is true that written tests are sometimes inappropriate or are misused, they are not the bogey that some persons fear, largely because they are not as universal or as controlling as uninformed critics often assume.

In contrast to the written-test phobia is the naive assumption that tests are infallible. It is strange what faith some people, in all innocence, have in the power and accuracy of written questions and answers. Ignoring the fact that the most perfect written tests can only measure a sampling of aptitude or knowledge, such persons seek to make the selection process overly dependent on this one tool. The disappointments, if not disasters, that flow from

19

such misguided efforts tend to discredit all testing—the good along with the bad; the limited, useful applications along with over-extended wholesale uses.

The Field of Competition. Finally, there should be a word said about the company within which the competition takes place. Under the early merit systems it was assumed that there would always be a plethora of candidates for public jobs. This led the pioneers in the new employment philosophy to forget about seeing to it that enough good candidates would apply. Not until the pinch of labor shortages began to be felt did public personnel agencies start aggressively to seek out prospective worthy applicants. Energetic, positive recruitment and concern for the attractions of the employment situation have now been widely accepted as necessary to elicit the interest of the best qualified prospects. Certainly unless recruitment measures attract the best available minds and skills, the staffing process consists of little more than a sorting out among the mediocre and the ill-qualified.

A look at some of the encrustations that have accumulated like barnacles on the walls of merit systems suggests that many a founding father or protector of the system was more bent upon keeping various categories of persons out of the service than in attracting an adequate supply of the best. The most blatant and short-sighted instance of this attitude has been the imposition of local residence requirements for employment. This "local-jobs-for-local-boys" type of thinking also gives away an underlying view of public jobs as some kind of welfare hand-out rather than as worthwhile positions deserving of the best talent that can be generated. Fortunately the pressure of the labor market, coupled with the growing variety of technical jobs for which local candidates could not always be found, have led to a gradual relaxation of this artificial and self-defeating constraint on the field of recruitment.

Still other arbitrary limitations illustrate unwise narrowing of the field—age, sex, and overly specific education-al prerequisites. Space does not permit an analysis of all of these, but we can say that the common denominator among all such restrictions has been a lack of relevance to the core objective: finding the individuals who showed the best potential for successful performance of the work. Some of these constraints, such as the requirement of citizenship, have caused little difficulty; others, such as veteran preference, have created controversy and eroded the merit principle. But there will be more to say about some of these subjects later with reference to certain issues of public policy that affect the personnel function.

Range of the Personnel Function

So far we have been directing attention to the initial focus of the merit idea—selection and entry into the service. There is much more to it than that, just as there is much more to the whole gamut of personnel operations, once an administrative machine is established and running. In fact, a few moments of reflection will demonstrate the breadth of the "people side" of management.

If we think of human beings as a major resource of any organization—either in terms of their intrinsic value or of their heterogeneity—we see immediately that we are dealing with the most important single aspect of the enterprise. Complex as they may be, neither the physical nor the fiscal sides of administration can match the human side in the range of issues that have to be faced, or in the prospects for good or bad results. The employees of any organization are the source of its creativity, its flavor, its style. No piece of equipment can replace human inventiveness; no balance sheet can reflect an enterprise's real status. Only its human components can determine whether the outfit is highly regarded by its clients or publics, is fulfilling the spirit of its mission, or is maintaining pace with its changing environment. Little argument is necessary therefore to see that nothing in public administration can be as significant in the long run as the acquisition, motivation, attitude, care, and performance of its manpower.

A bit of transitional thinking will give a clue to the variety of disciplines which are involved. In staffing—from initial entry to promotion and transfer—the field of psychological measurement is brought into play. Compensation decisions require economists and statisticians. Job analysis calls for skills in research and administrative procedure. Training draws upon adult education specialists and other occupations. Health and safety measures demand the employment of medical doctors, nurses, and safety engineers. Operating a retirement system necessitates expertise in the insurance field and actuarial mathematics. Dealing with employees corporately requires knowledge in labor relations. Interpretation of rules and adjudication of claims and complaints call for the skills of lawyers. And all the elements of leadership, supervision, incentive, evaluation, and discipline, on which the personnel program is expected to provide the principal guidance, can be fortified only by a liberal understanding of such social sciences as social psychology and sociology, to say nothing of a healthy dose of that conventional wisdom known as common sense.

This is not to say that the personnel specialist is or must be a paragon of expertise in all these fields; it is to say that the *function* of personnel administration requires bringing to bear skills and information from all these areas. And the personnel man must be the broker for bringing them together. It does mean that there is a weighty technical content in many aspects of managing manpower and that all government managers need to be familiar with the nature and scope of this content, for many of them must spend almost as much time making personnel decisions as do personnel specialists themselves. It also means that the views and information from a variety of specialized sources must be synthesized and reconciled in order to arrive at sensible personnel policy and practice.

The manager who thinks of personnel administration primarily as a procedural or legal matter fails to see the full implications of its aims and its insights. Society has no more difficult task than to identify its most gifted and capable members—whether for the purposes of selecting political leaders, determining educational achievement, or employing individuals in public services and business enterprises. The employment arena embraces all aspects of that selection process in its broadest sense, including appointment, assignment to a set duties, devising rewards, transferring to other tasks, developing talent, acquiring the satisfaction that comes from productive effort, and separating employees from the organization. Collectively, like social security, these are almost cradle-to-the-grave concerns.

The Network of Authority

Although the traditional terminology, borrowed from the military, appears to be dying out, vestiges of the once irreconcilable differences between "line" and "staff" activities still plague the administrative scene. The classical definition of line operations describes them as segments of the program for which the organization was created: production of a product or rendering a service, dealing with clientele groups, decision-making, and exercising the necessary supervisory command to give effect to these operations. Staff work, on the other hand, is supposed to consist of planning, research, advisory services, and absence of command. Functions concerned with the internal administration of an enterprise, including personnel management, were usually thought of as staff.

Intersecting Specializations

Long ago, this author (and others) contended that so-called staff activities concerned with internal organization affairs (such as budgeting, methods analysis, and personnel) were simply specialized functions, albeit internal, no different in importance or in power status from the so-called line activities. This view held that organizations could be more readily pictured as networks or grids of authority, rather than as charts with solid lines for "line" and dotted lines for "staff" functions. In the network approach some lines are vertical, emanating from the chief executive and representing the program activities; others are horizontal, also emanating from the same executive source, but in addition intersecting the horizontal program lines and representing the staff functions. The point is that both types of function are equally important; each contains elements of command as well as advice; both are merely specialized aspects of the total mission of the enterprise, and it is idle to insist that a staff function is necessarily subordinate.

This revised theory was designed to counter a common contention, still sometimes heard, that such activities as the personnel function exist only as a service to the line, in spite of the fact that across-the-board personnel policies may have been sanctioned by law or were the dictates of the chief executive. Program supervisors down the line—having been led to believe that the requirements or controls were really "services"—were prone to assume that they could ignore them, or that the staff specialists in the executive offices need not be listened to. They overlooked the facts that there might be elements of command as well as advice in the staff man's interpretations and that he was an arm of the chief executive in his field as much as the program man was in his.

In short, the roles of line and staff functions were being blown up as antithetical; and the program function, no matter how small it actually was, was elevated to a sacrosanct position of superiority over any staff function, no matter how weighty and pervasive. This attitude exacerbated natural conflicts between departmental and organization-wide views and promoted little islands of independence which undercut cohesion and coordination. Issuing dog licenses, simply because it is a line program, is not necessarily more important than maintaining a rational city-wide pay policy. Nor is predicting the weather necessarily more essential to government-wide purposes than insuring healthy mobility among key personnel.

Reconciliation Necessary

Whenever a line operator's interpretation of his interests appears to run afoul of some organization-wide policy or practice, there should be some effort at reconciliation rather than an assumption that the overall policy must bend to the desires of the localized interest. If the objectives that are seemingly in conflict are all accepted as valid orders of the top command, reconciliation is more feasible than if one of the objectives is presumed to have no real power behind it.

Line and staff functions—and their protagonists—may suffer from the narrowness, the myopia, the prejudice of specialization. But staff, such as personnel management, has no corner on these characteristics; if anything, they are more likely to be found among those who have stayed too long in some specialized program function that is only one part of an organization's mission. At least, the staff functionaries tend to have a more Olympian view of the total enterprise, albeit they too can suffer from pettifogging and administrative blindness.

A Balanced View

In any event, it has seemed more contributory to organizational health to look upon any pair of line and staff activities as equal channels of direction: one specializing in part of the organization's end purposes and concerned with some particular outside clientele; and the other one specializing in part of the methodology of running the organization and concerned with certain inside clientele.

In addition, there is the fact that once an organization is in existence it takes on purposes beyond those for which it was initially created. It may have been set up to collect revenue, but it soon develops quite a collection of other obligations and responsibilities derived from its environment and related activities. Having assembled a body of employees, it takes on, like all units of society, some obligations that previously did not exist. The community comes to have an interest in its behavior as an employer. Its employment policy, treatment of its workers, lay-off practices, and pay scales, become as critical to the organization's acceptance—perhaps even its existence—as does the quality of its product or service. We need only to mention the possibility of employee strikes to drive this point home.

In government employment in particular the public has as much of an interest and stake in *how* a program is carried out as in *what* program is undertaken. The *how* factor is the essence of most staff activities, especially applicable to personnel policy and procedure.

The Executive's Positive Role

Stating this fact of life is not designed to scare off the government manager on the grounds that his personnel responsibilities are awesome and somehow incompatible with his operating duties. It does impose the obligation (as mentioned in the first chapter) that he try to see his special operating function in reasonable relation to others, including those that require him to follow certain rules of the game, those that deal with the *how* factor. He must weigh continuously what he deems to be the welfare of his special cause in the context of the cause of the total organization, so that he behaves as much as a judge as he does as an advocate.

Power Over Personnel Action

But even more significantly, he needs to see his role as a positive one. His personnel responsibilities, when conscientiously carried out, are more likely to be an asset than a liability. If he looks upon his duty as a welcome challenge, if he appreciates the reasons for and abides by the features of personnel policy that are sound in terms of the over-all organizational good and are responsive to democratic control, his voice will be influential in changing those features that are unsound, outmoded, or not really serving the public interest.

What's more, the lion's share of the personnel function is within his control. His is the decision as to what jobs shall be created and who shall carry what responsibility. These decisions may have a whole chain of consequences, but they are his decisions. He estimates his manpower needs, and he is the chief diagnostician as to needs for training, what kind, and when. He has the most important single influence on evaluation of performance, on the use of special pay flexibilities and awards, and on productivity. His example and his ability to motivate others count most in winning the enthusiastic response of employees to organization goals.

Some personnel policies may seem remote from the executive's concerns. The substantive content of various fringe benefits (usually requiring legislative action), the provisions of the retirement system, and the like, seldom

27

come within his purview, although he should be sufficiently familiar with them to be a first source of counsel when employees have questions or express concern.

Influencing General Policy

Some supervisory officials assume that they have no part to play in arrangements for recruiting or in the design of examinations. However, if they do not, it is usually their own fault. Government managers who show an interest and have constructive ideas about such matters are almost invariably called upon to help. Progressive personnel agencies not only welcome but require the assistance of knowledgeable leaders in the various program fields in determining qualification standards, the best criteria for predicting success, and useful examination components. In addition, they can be of immense help in recruitment, in persuading potential applicants to get into the competition. No one can interest a young engineer in the work of an organization as well as an experienced engineer; and an economist is likely to be the most effective recruiter of other economists.

All the obligations and opportunities for participation in the human side of enterprise will be even more evident as our exploration of the subject unfolds in succeeding chapters. But one concept that the government manager might well be convinced of at the start is this: in democratic government, in any system of service to the public, there is a natural concern by that public not only in *what* functions are performed but in *how* they are performed and especially *how people are used* to promote that performance. This in essence is what public personnel administration is all about.

3

Organizing
and Assigning Work

WHEN THOSE in charge of government programs
make the daily decisions affecting the assignment of
tasks to their subordinates, they seldom think of the implications for personnel purposes. Understandably, they
are so engrossed in the operating program implications of
assignment that they may well overlook that they are also
contributing to the personnel climate of the organization
and that they are shaping the conditions which will make
the next episode of assignment easier or more difficult.

How the sub functions of an activity are organized and
related to each other, how the talents of employees are
used, what delegations are made, what reviews are provided for, the clearances insisted upon, the setting of dead-
lines, the reaction of the manager to his subordinates'
ideas, the quality of a service expected—these are certainly
all facets of substantive decision-making and parts of what
we call the operating job. The manager would not consider them matters in which the personnel officials have a

direct concern, and he would be absolutely right. That is the very point; they are almost wholly within the personal jurisdiction of the line manager. But the decisions have everything to do with motivation, the demands made on the labor market, job classification, and the costs of administration.

The only issue is whether these decisions are being made with full awareness of their impact on administration in general and especially on the personnel front. No matter how much a government official or supervisor may protest that he has little or nothing to do with personnel policy or practice, in his organizing and assigning functions alone he is making or profoundly influencing such policy and exemplifying such practice.

Work and Motivation

Most government managers need not be told about the exhilaration that comes from facing challenging tasks and meeting responsibilities that require use of every talent or capacity one possesses. What they sometimes overlook is that the work itself can be just as satisfying to their subordinates, that its power as a motivator is applicable to everybody.

Theory X and Theory Y

A number of years ago Douglas McGregor—keen analyst of the industrial scene and master of psychological research findings—observed that management had traditionally been hobbled by the notion that people only worked because they had to and that a combination of rewards and punishments, the "carrot" and the "stick," had to be employed to get them to produce. He called this "Theory X". The theory failed to take into account that man is an achieving animal by nature. That is, he finds it necessary to be productively occupied, secures satisfaction out of achieving, and finds his prime motivation in work. This being true, he need not be cajoled into working; he need only be persuaded that what he is doing is as useful and satisfying to him as it is to his employer. This approach is, in effect, McGregor's "Theory Y".

This thesis about what motivates men is not new. Those who have thought more than superficially about the subject know that work can even be fun, that it is really the ultimate form of recreation. Psychologists have merely confirmed what many of us know from personal experience. Yet, the tendency has been to assume that our colleagues have to be driven even if we ourselves do not.

In addition to any lessons that this theory may have for a style of supervision, it clearly has great implications for the organization and assignment of duties. If an employee's basic emotional needs are at least in major part served by his sense of achievement, then the more meaning the work has for him the more likely it will serve that need. Conversely, the more routinized, dull, or irrelevant his tasks are—in relation to his capacity—the less they can contribute to his satisfaction and his desire to continue to perform.

Work Attractions

Most public programs have a built-in advantage in this respect; their purposes are focused on the general public welfare. Because they serve the entire population—whether in a city, a state, or the nation—they are usually of considerable magnitude in comparison with related activities in the private sector. The competing demands, the imponderables in most public issues, the sheer complexity of serving the public interest create challenges that are seldom equalled in other pursuits. Many publicly-operated enterprises illustrate the point: public school administration,

31

maintenance of law and order, international negotiations, exploration of space, regulation of the economy, to name only a few. In other words, there is much job satisfaction to be derived from governmental activities simply because they are what they are—provided unwise organization and controls do not deprive workers of all that may be gained from this natural advantage.

To those young people who genuinely wish to identify themselves with endeavors that serve others, that extend beyond money-making, the public service offers infinite opportunity. But we must make certain that the spirit of service is intelligently exploited and encouraged. Persons with high ideals are alienated from government in general if their experience in government employment leaves them frustrated and cynical. They want a part of the action and, given the requisite amount of competence, they should be encouraged to exercise as much latitude as possible.

The same may be said for all age groups and all gradations of skill. The most productive (and probably the happiest) human being is one who is called upon to apply every talent he possesses, to extend his capacity to the fullest. Obviously not every individual requires the stimulus of the very top positions to reach this optimum point, but few are content to work for an extended period much below their highest skills. The aim of a good personnel program, and therefore the aim of every conscientious supervisor, is to maintain the conditions that will evoke from each worker the best that is within his power.

Applying the Theory

The old so-called scientific management school of thought (it was really only pseudo-scientific), preoccupied as it was with mechanization, job routinization, and stopwatches, did contribute to improved engineering of mass production but in the process almost reduced the man on the assembly line to a mindless automaton. The newer social science, based on the assumption that man needs to tax his capacity, has moved away from job simplification (except to make use of and develop low-skilled laborers). It has sought to enlarge jobs wherever practicable, even making posts on assembly lines as broad, varied, and challenging as physically possible.

The Human Side of Assignment. In sub-dividing and assigning tasks the manager needs to be conscious of their relationship to personal capacities and development in each individual case. Keeping jobs as meaningful as they can practically be should be the main goal. Some of the measures that may be considered are these:

1. Diversifying tasks in any one unit as much as feasible.
2. Delegating authority to each layer in the hierarchy to the maximum extent consistent with the clarity of policy guides, training of staff, and the effectiveness of post-audit procedures.
3. Assigning whole integrals of functions to individuals or units instead of splitting them into fine specializations with separate employees or groups concentrating on each.
4. Permitting workers to follow through on tasks or projects from start to finish rather than carry out single segments of the process.
5. Training employees to grow beyond the tasks they have been performing.
6. Making use of project teams or task forces.
7. Rotating employees from time to time among different assignments in order to give them the flavor and stimulus of new experiences and challenges.

Such techniques are useful in eliciting wholehearted employee participation in getting the job done, whether they apply to processing tax returns, directing traffic, reading meters, surveying rights-of-way, making medical examinations, conducting research, inspecting food, or adjudicating claims.

Faith in People. Note that there is a common denominator running through all of these methods: they are built upon an abiding faith in people. They assume that employees really want to achieve, provided they are convinced that what they are doing is worthwhile and are given enough latitude to do it responsibly. When they are trusted and expected to do a complete job, they are likely to respond with their best effort. When it is assumed that they will resist responsibility and are entrusted only with uninteresting segments of tasks, they are likely to respond in kind, with half-hearted results.

The American Telephone and Telegraph Company has conducted some experiments in recent years that support this thesis. In what was termed a "job enrichment" program, AT&T held environmental and reward factors constant while systematically improving tasks for experimental groups of workers. Those groups were given more chance than the others for achievement, recognition, responsibility, challenge, and growth, and they almost invariably surpassed the rest in productivity, quality of customer service, attendance, and keeping costs down. Another result was that management discovered new sources for managerial upgrading.

Some Limitations. In government establishments, problems of accountability and insuring uniform administration may make delegation of authority more difficult. Legislative bodies, in their anxiety to maintain control, tend to overprescribe procedure and to be intolerant of decision or action by anyone less than the "top man". Citizens and their representatives will continue to demand review of some actions by headquarters or by higher echelon officials, regardless of the advantage of relying more fully on civil servants in field offices or other lower levels in the hierarchy. However, without denying the need for bureaucratic accountability, it must be acknowledged that most government offices still have plenty of room for further delegation for authority to make decisions. The more common reasons for holding the reins tight at central points may be found in the absence of sound criteria for decentralized action and of adequate training, but most of all in a lack of basic trust in the staff.

It may also be claimed that automation, especially data processing, complicates efforts to place more challenging tasks in lower level jobs. But, here too, the fact must be faced that for every job that has been made meaningless by the introduction of machines, at least two new ones demanding higher skills seem to be created. The development of the staff to take on new and more complex tasks is the obvious solution.

Whatever the obstacles, the relevance to employee motivation of organizing work and making assignments seems perfectly clear. It is an area in which the government manager has the fewest restrictions on his own latitude and in which he may have the most profound influence on the productivity and quality of performance of his staff.

Responding to the Labor Market

Many an otherwise-sophisticated public executive tends to look upon both the combinations of duties that make up jobs and the status of the labor market as inexorable, fixed entities. He is inclined to accept what has gone before, or what the high priests of occupational specializations have ordained, as the inevitable way the positions in his enterprise must be organized. He also assumes that the skills needed to perform them are always ready-made in the labor market. It is the convenient, least-upsetting posture one can take—that is, unless the stark reality of being

35

unable to fill the jobs or the realization that they are not being performed well brings one up short.

Breaking with Tradition

As a matter of fact, most managers can accommodate to both external and internal conditions beyond their direct control by the simple expedient of re-examining the manner in which duties and tasks have been combined for the attention of individual workers. The medical profession has already demonstrated how duties can be reorganized to make fuller use of nurses and other paramedical personnel, thereby reducing the demand for scarce doctors —although there is still much room for progress in this regard. Many establishments employing engineers, accountants, technicians, skilled tradesmen, economists, and so forth, have failed to learn from the medical experience. Even the relatively new field of computer programming has gotten off to a bad start by over-structuring what things must be done by which people with what titles. The worst offenders historically are the blue-collar trades and crafts which jealously guard who has the right to use what tools on which materials in whose projects.

Whatever good reasons may have supported time-worn insistence on fixed combinations of tasks as occupational requisites, they do not fit an age of change, an age of technology, an age of both frustrating labor shortages and oversupply. The basic characteristic of the labor market in this and many other countries is one that is likely to continue for a long time: a long-range, though fluctuating, shortage of persons with the higher skills, and an excess of those with little or no skills at all. It is this reality that the manager must face up to. Shortages and overages exist not only in terms of supply but in terms of demand. The manager can influence that demand by the way he combines duties into jobs.

The traditional pattern of tasks assigned to one person—known as a job—does not ordinarily take into account the availability of individuals who have the particular combinations of knowledges and skills necessary to perform in that job. To be sure, some occupations (like those of teachers and brick masons) have been of long standing; and the educational system and other influences on the supply side have accommodated to the situation, almost automatically producing ready-made artisans and experts to fit the bill.

But jobs as well as technology evolve; and government in particular has needs for kinds of work that have few or no counterparts in the rest of the economy, such as police duties, revenue collection, military support, natural resource conservation and management, diplomacy, highway design and maintenance, and many others. The growth of public functions has put special strain on finding the man power to carry on these functions peculiar to government. Likewise, government shares with industry the agonies of perennial shortages in the whole range of professional and managerial occupations. A few years ago the Municipal Manpower Commission cited in dramatic terms the alarmingly great unmet needs for administrative and professional personnel in American cities.

Conscious Job Design

The obligation on government managers is inescapable. They cannot afford to follow traditional patterns; they must not make their task-setting determinations in a vacuum, isolated from what other parts of government or society in general are doing. In short, as they organize work, they must think of the best ways to concentrate as much of the higher-skill duties in as few of the jobs as possible.

This responsibility is the essence of job design. It

means knowing which tasks are of a higher order of complexity and which are of a lesser; it means careful job analysis and study of the labor supply; it means reconciling these considerations with the necessities of serving the public and maintaining acceptable levels of performance. And above all, it means a willingness to try new approaches and abandon reliance on pre-packaged jobs as the inexorable units of management. Obviously, when more higher duties are concentrated in fewer jobs, more intermediate and lower-skill jobs will be created; it is this result that accommodates to the shortages and overages of the market. The balance can never be perfect, but deliberate design of jobs to approximate this objective can go far to maintain a balance between supply and demand.

Conscious job design can also serve a noble social purpose in these trying times. One of America's great problems is the existence of an abnormally large number of persons who are unemployed or under-employed because of lack of job skills and orientation to the world of work. A shredding out of routine duties from high-skill jobs can make it possible to establish more low-demand or trainee-type spots in which persons with such limitations can be employed. It should be recognized that studies have shown that the more routine the tasks the less likely it is that persons with high skills can perform them successfully; whereas routine work may be entirely satisfying to people who are not equipped for greater responsibilities—and actually be more efficiently performed by them.

Relation to Motivation

This brings us to the question of whether what is being said here squares with what was said earlier about the effect of work on motivation. Superficially it may appear that the two concepts are not consistent, but closer examination suggests otherwise. Concentrating higher duties may result in fewer jobs requiring the highest skills, but for such jobs that do exist there is no reason why what has been said about faith in people, delegation, and task enlargement would not be applicable. In fact, all the more so. The impact of job enrichment on the most highly trained and gifted people on the staff is likely to be the most marked.

At the same time, job enrichment can also be applicable to the most menial jobs. Granted that such jobs may be created purposely to demand very little of their incumbents, once they are successfully performed the potential of still better performance, following deliberate task improvement, is always present. Also, even the simplest of work can be made meaningful. The tasks of a housekeeper contain much menial drudgery, but together they add up to a responsible job of maintenance and may even entail using a flair for decoration and artistry. A custodian in a public building does not have to be expert at any trade, but he can be made to feel responsible for the general appearance of a place.

The key lies in delegating responsibility for results and in allowing latitude in method. Cleaning up a school classroom can be a hated chore if every step is prescribed, if each instrument used is over-standardized, and if the sequence of tasks is determined by someone other than the worker. In contrast, if the individual is encouraged to develop his own regimen, select the cleaning agents, determine the instruments and methods to be used, perhaps even indulge in some minor touching up and decorative activities—all within suitable constraints as to cost, of course—he has room in which to develop some pride in what he is doing. If the expectations on the job are described to him in terms of results desired; if it is made clear that he is accountable for achieving those results but may use his own ingenuity as to how he goes about it; if the stress is on how well he succeeded in meeting those

39

goals rather than on his conformance to petty methodology prescribed by someone who may never have performed the work—in those circumstances the chances are that he will find the duty meaningful and put his whole heart into doing his best. He will readily sense that the appearance of that classroom and that school building will be what it is because of his decisions and dedication, his inventiveness and carefulness, his industry and perseverance.

Job design to accommodate to the labor market is entirely compatible with the principle that man does not work for bread alone, that he gets one of the major satisfactions in life out of work, and that his performance will be commensurate with the meaning that he finds in it.

Assignment and Job Classification

Still another effect flowing from the way in which the government executive sorts out and assigns work is in the classification of positions on the basis of duties and responsibilities. Because this is such a basic—to say nothing of being an often misunderstood and sometimes abused— aspect of the personnel function, a few words of background are in order.

How Job Classification Came About

The idea of analyzing jobs, evaluating them, and arranging them into classes based on common characteristics of kind and level of duties and knowledge and skill required is an American invention. It was a response in the early part of this century to the chaotic conditions of work assignment and pay that were rampant in our public services. Job evaluation has also come to be widely used in industry as well as at all levels of government, although in a substantial variety of forms.

Prior to the advent of the position classification idea, pay for government employees was determined either by rigid line-items in legislative appropriations or by haphazard executive fiat. The result had little to do with what people did or the worth of their services. Difficult work was often paid less than routine work. Supervisors sometimes made less money than their subordinates. Employees doing identical duties seldom were in the same pay category. Little wonder that a movement under the banner "equal pay for equal work"—with its roots going back to complaints registered as long ago as the mid-nineteenth century—began getting attention just before World War I.

Meanwhile, private industry was feeling the pressure of competition and seeking new ways to foster efficiency. Its prime motivation was to analyze jobs in order to discover the optimum ways to improve production, with cognizance also of the potential advantages of standardization of employees' pay.

The answer to the pressures both for equal pay for equal work and for efficient organization of work processes was the same: a rational identification and arrangement of positions in terms of what they involved, what they demanded of incumbents, and what they were worth to the employer. And so job evaluation and classification was born, with its concomitant feature of standardized pay schedules geared to the classification schemes.

Other countries, except for Canada, were slow to adopt the idea. However, in recent decades more and more nations are moving toward the American practice. The older civil services of Great Britain and continental Europe had systems of their own that comported with the stratified societies of which they were a part. Generally, these consisted of cadres of employees, each representing a broad educational and social level, with members of each group privileged to hold certain broad categories of posts. As these corps systems evolved, they came to represent different degrees of privilege and prestige depending on education and social standing. Actual duties were seldom considered as important.

The American plan was distinctly more democratic; and eventually its advantages became clear, at least in comparison with any of the other forms of personnel structure that had been contrived. By the 1950s and 1960s many countries were seriously questioning the viability of their corps systems and turning to modifications that gave more attention to the duties of jobs, to equating the qualifications of employees with those duties, and to pay commensurate with the duties.

Some Myths and Truths

By its nature the classification of positions requires a certain amount of central control. If like jobs are to be treated alike with respect to recruitment, pay, and other considerations, the classifications must be consistent. This means common standards by which the determinations are made, consistent practices in making the judgments, and opportunity for post-audit of actions taken. Obviously, completely independent determinations by each operating manager would not be likely to lead to consistent interpretations in an area such as the evaluation of positions where so many permutations and refinements are likely to come into play. No unit of administration is as susceptible to variety and change as that galaxy of duties called a "position". Where similar jobs exist in more than one office, it is especially necessary that consistent evaluations be made.

Except for this fundamental principle, position classification systems can be of a substantial variety. Like the concept of merit system itself, classification should be thought rather as an objective than as a specific procedure. Thus, particular practices or interpretations in any one civil service jurisdiction are not necessarily indicative of the system in principle.

There are some popular misconceptions about the classification process that need to be laid to rest, such as: that the way to change pay scales is to upgrade positions instead of squarely facing the need to revise the scales themselves; that the process requires lengthy, labored job descriptions; that decisions on classification can be made only by some inside-track priesthood; that a job is a never-changing collection of duties and that classifications once set are immutable; and that the criteria and standards by which determinations are made are laid down without relevance to the real world of what occupations and government offices require. If any of these conditions exist in actuality, they do not represent what a classification system is supposed to be or how it is to operate. Too often the tendency is to let the system itself take the rap for the sins of poor administration.

Essentially, all a classification system can profess to be is a means whereby all jobs are grouped into broad occupational categories and then subdivided into levels of difficulty and responsibility. The criteria are these:

- the kind of work and the knowledge and skills necessary to perform it.
- the latitude with which the work is carried out.
- the degree of control and review exercised with respect to the product.
- the consequences of the work, or the responsibility it carries.
- the degree to which direction of the work of others is entailed.
- the ultimate accountability and relationship to other activities that are involved.

A pay system is a separate matter, attached and geared to the classification scheme but not an integral part of it.

This point is best clarified by observing that the classification of an occupation or an individual position can be changed without affecting the pay system, and schedules of compensation can be revised without changing the classification structure.

So much for a sketchy background to define our terms and make sure that the writer and the reader are talking about the same thing.

The Manager's Role

The important issue for purposes of this volume is what the average government manager has to do with all this. We have already noted how influential his determinations as to work assignments can be on motivation and productivity and on making use of the labor market. These same determinations are just as critical with reference to the classification of positions.

It should be the *real* duties of a position—whether vacant or occupied—that are classified, not some imaginary ones that do not exist in reality. Yet, it is also true that not all the functions of a position may be performed at once or within a limited cycle of time, and are not therefore observable on any given day. Some duties have to be anticipated.

In any event, it is the government manager who decides what a position shall be, what duties it shall contain, now and tomorrow, and what reliance shall be placed on the actions and judgments of its incumbent. The manager may get advice from several quarters—the budget experts, the organization and methods analysts, or the personnel specialists—but the final decision is his.

Entering into the decision may be considerations relating to how the classification of the position might turn out; and there is nothing illegitimate about this per se. The problem arises when a manager lets such a concern be the *prime* consideration affecting his assignment of duties. Nothing relating to this subject deserves more emphasis than this point: the ultimate controlling factor in structuring positions should be solely the effectiveness of these arrangements in serving the mission of the organization.

It should hardly be necessary to stress this elementary precept to the operating official who has his program interests at heart. Yet it is often one of those making the loudest protests (about alleged obstructions caused by the classification system or its agents) who does not hesitate to manipulate assignments to get a raise for an employee, with little regard for the impact on his program. Such an action is seldom less than deleterious:

- it takes the short-sighted view, focusing on one job and one employee, without taking into account the effect on others.
- it overlooks the most efficient arrangement of duties as to work sequence, review processes, quality factors, and the like.
- it may create a chain of demands from other employees which the supervisor will have no rational grounds in resisting and which will utterly upset any reasonable organizational structure.
- it ignores the motivational effects of job structuring.
- it makes replacement more difficult whenever the incumbent of the artificially-inflated job leaves.

What has been said here should not be taken to mean that either jobs or their classifications should be static. Good position classification is always a dynamic affair, an instrument that is responsive to all legitimate changes in function, organization, or assignment. Genuine changes in or evolution of positions, when they are more than peripheral or minor, demand appropriate and prompt changes in classification. But the accent is on legitimacy and genuineness.

Program managers have a right to expect the classification system to be dynamic—but only to meet real program needs, not trumped-up emergencies. The wise and far-sighted executive does not fall for spurious techniques. Even if he were tempted to exploit them, he knows that invariably they will backfire—usually on his own operation. He recognizes that once deviation from program welfare as the controlling principle occurs, his own activity —to say nothing of the rest of the organization—reaps the whirlwind of inequity, demoralization, and poor performance.

Opportunities and Constraints

In a more constructive vein, attention should be drawn to several ways in which government managers can participate most profitably in the classification process.

Class Standards. First, and most basic, are the developing of occupational definitions, demarking one field from another, setting the qualifications needed for effective performance, and developing criteria for distinguishing different levels within a field. The products of these steps are variously called guides, standards, or class specifications.

The prime unit is the *class:* a group of positions (existing or anticipated) that are sufficiently similar in nature and level of duties, responsibilities, and qualifications required to warrant similar treatment for purposes of recruitment, examination, layoff practices, or pay. Each occupation consists of several such classes. Classes of comparable level in related occupations may be treated horizontally as a *grade,* with a common range of pay rates, or each class may have its own pay range.

Development of the definitions of these classes, so that they may serve as useful criteria for the allocation of individual positions to classes, calls for the expert knowledge of those who work daily in each occupational field. Panels of operating officials are commonly the experts who can best perform this function. Analysts and writers from the personnel establishment can serve as leaders, coordinators, and implementers; but they are necessarily heavily dependent upon the insights, wisdom, and integrity of the program managers for technical judgments as to the comparability of various operations, the relative complexity or difficulty of functions or processes, and the knowledges and skills necessary to perform them. In any well-run classification program, interested and qualified managers are not only intimately involved in the initial development of standards concepts and criteria but are also called upon to appraise draft statements of them before publication.

Work on the standards is the most fundamental way in which program executives can exercise a constructive influence on the manner in which position classification is carried out. The decisions reflected in the standards established have a continuing impact on all evaluations and judgments made thereafter.

Such standards are, of course, subject to change, especially as occupations or program content changes. For example, if new responsibilities gradually accrue to hospital aides as a group, or if social case workers take on added decision-making as the result of new legislative provisions, the effect must be appraised and reflected in the standards for the whole occupation. Each such potential change is an occasion for consultation and active participation of operating officials. Under these circumstances, when they later find flaws in the criteria, they must acknowledge that the mistakes were of their own making; and they will have to share the responsibility for correction.

Spotting Job Evolution. Only the most mechanized and standardized of jobs remain static. In meeting today's rapidly shifting needs the work of individuals in the professions, in managerial support activities, and in technical jobs of various kinds tends to evolve. A job created on paper last year may not have developed as expected; it may turn out to be more or less of a job.

Likewise, the particular talents of incumbents can have a profound effect on what the position turns out to be. One man may fulfill expectations routinely; another may fall short and perform only part of the job; still another may take on additional tasks, merit the reliance of his bosses in certain ways, or otherwise add to the job sufficiently that it becomes in effect a new job with larger dimensions than originally planned. This is especially true in the case of one-of-a-kind jobs. The only person in a position to spot such developments as they occur and to be sure of their impact is the supervisory official in charge. It is his responsibility, in fact, to be ever alert to *all* job changes—whether caused by individual talents, program changes, or organizational shifts—and to report those changes so that job re-evaluation can be readily undertaken.

This approach to job change is a far cry from the dishonest and hazardous tactic of falsifying jobs or deliberately padding duties in order to gratify a favorite son— a reprehensible practice which has already been sufficiently condemned. Instead, we are talking about the legitimate dynamism that almost invariably occurs in any live-wire organization and the positive responsibility of supervisors to observe and report such developments. Implicit in this discussion, of course, is the responsibility of the managers to make sure that they approve of the changes that have evolved. They are not the prisoners of conditions that may have unintentionally developed. Before deciding on the nature of changes and the need to report them for re-evaluation, they must first decide whether these developments are consistent with program aims, with other operations in the division, and with good management in general. Especially when a job becomes vacant, the supervisor must be mindful of any characteristics that were peculiar to the last incumbent and must not necessarily project these into the future.

In any event, the role of the manager in job evolution is very real; it is not only useful, it is irreplaceable.

Deciding Specific Classifications. The best-run systems —by no means all—incorporate a large measure of participation by supervisors in the very process of evaluation of jobs. This does not mean letting each supervisor classify all the jobs under his supervision, independently of the rest of the organization. Unless every such leader had perfect knowledge of jobs in every other part of the organization and were able to discount his own, such a process would amount to little more than the chaos that existed before classification plans were invented.

What it does mean is drawing upon the skills of responsible managers in helping make the difficult, sometimes controversial, judgments about classifying individual jobs that must be made every day. This may be done by having panels of supervisory officials decide particularly complex cases or hear appeals from employees or other managers on contested decisions. Or individual executives may be called upon to advise personnel officials where some of the determining factors are technical or especially difficult to fathom.

The program manager can be as fair and judicious as anyone else when he understands the jobs in question and the criteria to be applied; but he is in the best position to be judicious when he is not a party directly at interest. For those cases under his personal jurisdiction he is expected, of course, to form a judgment and make a recommendation. However, he does not occupy an Olympian vantage point—seeing all sides and relationships—that would permit final determinations on his own proposals.

49

Some Limitations. It is quite true, then, that there are some constraints on the manager's prerogatives when it comes to position classification. These limitations are inherent in maintaining like allocations of like jobs in different subdivisions of the organization. They are implicit in assuring equal pay for equal work and in guaranteeing rational and economic forms of organization.

The competent manager, confident in the integrity and wisdom of his own ideas and plans, does not fear or resent legitimate controls on his authority. He knows that he can "sell" the virtues of what is needed to advance his mission, especially when he demonstrates that he also appreciates the missions of other parts of the organization, including the possibility that they may sometimes outclass his own in importance or urgency.

He is all the more confident when he has had a part in the design and operation of the entire classification system. When he has participated in developing standards; when he realizes how much his own choices in assigning duties bear upon classification results; when he has had to take some of the responsibility for making tough and borderline decisions—in such circumstances he identifies with the classification process instead of viewing it as an alien force.

Assuming that an enlightened personnel program exists, the manager's own behavior and performance go a long way to insure his influence on the entire process. Even if personnel program leadership is unimaginative or otherwise wanting, the integrity and constructive counsel of good managers can help bring about change in the right direction. Outright rejection of the techniques of job analysis only deprives the manager of the many valuable by-products it affords: helping to plan workflow and organization, spot duplications and gaps in performance, and plan expenditures and budgets.

Speaking of budgets suggests the appropriateness of a final section of this chapter on the subject of economy.

Keeping Costs Down

Personnel and fiscal policy and controls are too often considered as separate and distinct worlds of concern. Yet there are numerous points at which these two managerial areas intersect and become almost indistinguishable. One such area is in the creation and structuring of positions and in the classifying (or pricing) of those positions. Other facets of personnel practice have great impact on the economical operation of an enterprise—such as the quality of its work-force, the motivation and performance of that work-force, and the degree to which deadwood and incompetence are forthrightly dealt with—but nothing has a more direct and influential bearing on costs than the whole job-content area just discussed. Considering that payroll costs are as much as seventy or eighty percent of state and local government operating budgets (not considering capital outlay), few items can match them for potential economy.

The first observation that deserves emphasis in this connection is this: all the precepts of good position classification, all the do's and don't's regarding job design and duties assignment, are completely consistent with keeping costs of operation within rational bounds. Being mindful of the impact of work assignments and responsibility on motivation and productivity can have enormous significance for economical operation of public agencies. Constructing jobs to accommodate to the shortages and overages of the labor market (possibly resulting in decreases in the proportion of higher-grade jobs) may mean considerable economy, especially in jurisdictions where payrolls constitute the bulk of the expenditures. Keeping classifications accurate and current and avoiding the excesses and misuses of the system can certainly prevent unnecessary waste and extravagance.

In addition, one specific malpractice requires special mention—the tendency to spread higher-grade duties in small proportions over as many jobs as possible in order to acquire as many higher grades as possible.

Such a device may be necessary where jobs are geographically separated and where each must contain the full range of functions from the most complex to the simplest. For such cases the general rule has been established of allocating positions on the basis of the highest duties called for. But to deliberately spread such duties around in order to achieve grades violates every precept of good management and is very costly. Such an abuse of a sound classification principle designed for unusual cases does not comport with the organization of tasks to fit employees' capacities and induce the greatest job satisfaction. It completely ignores the effects on recruitment and the labor market. And, most of all, it is a plain, unadulterated waste of public funds.

Another misapplication of the classification concept is the arbitrary ranking of supervisory positions on the basis of numbers of persons supervised. This is the lazy way to judge the value of jobs. The magnitude and importance of work is not necessarily reflected in the size of a staff. To make size a controlling criterion also has the disadvantage of tempting supervisors to make staff expansion a cardinal objective regardless of real need, a condition hardly contributing to economy.

The rational development and faithful application of a classification plan is as likely to insure an economical operation as any one device employed in management. What's more, the technique of job analysis can serve other organizational purposes—beyond insuring a reasonable and equitable scheme for grouping, filling, and pricing positions—which also help to induce economy.

The government manager is unknown who does not at least talk the game of running a tight ship, of providing a service at the lowest possible cost. If he is sincere, if he understands his trade—and wishes to curb his own weaknesses and overcome his shortcomings—he will welcome the opportunities and the constraints provided by position classification as a tool of management. He will, in other words, use his latitude and his authority in organization and in work assignment to comport with his laudable goal of economically-operated public services.

4

Keeping Up Manpower

THE EXTENT of latitude of the individual government manager in shaping jobs requires more elucidation than argument; his role in the acquisition of manpower has not been as clear. In fact, the impression is still harbored in many quarters that this aspect of personnel administration is somehow beyond his pale, that it is the exclusive province of the personnel specialists, civil service commissioners, and their entourage. However, the wise administrator does not sit idly by, feeling sorry for himself, as the prisoner of an alien recruiting and examining system. He injects himself into the act. Nor does the able personnel man resent this participation as an intrusion; he welcomes it as a bona fide help. The not-so-able personnel man desperately needs it.

There are various points at which the operating administrator plays a key role in attracting, acquiring, and placing manpower in his part of the government establishment: planning for the kinds and numbers of personnel needed, stirring up good prospects, fostering genuine competition, facilitating the movement and advancement of people, practicing a policy of ready release of employees, and assisting in the selection process itself. At every one of these points his participation and attitudes are crucial to the success of personnel recruitment and placement policy.

The underlying assumption of this chapter is that we are dealing with keeping posts filled by either outside recruitment or internal transfer and promotion. The tendency to look upon these facets of the personnel function as relatively unrelated processes is a mistake. The objective, after all, is the same: to get the best qualified person but in such a manner that all those worthy of consideration get adequate attention. The difference is only in source and methods. Whether the recruitment field is the entire nation, the community, or a government jurisdiction, the same basic purpose must govern the procedures and techniques that are used. When candidates come primarily from within the organization, the details are different but the principles are the same. These principles, set forth in Chapter 2, will be further elaborated in this chapter, with some related subjects carrying over into the later chapter on "Some Public Policies to Live With".

Planning the Work-force

If administrative success depends in the last analysis on the quality of the people engaged in administration, then everything that goes into a rational recruitment and selection policy we would expect to be operation-oriented. Certainly those features of personnel policy which focus on quality factors are designed for the good of public administration as a whole, but some of the encrustations and barnacles that have accumulated around merit systems seem remote from such a grand purpose. This is particularly true of arbitrary requirements imposed by legislative bodies in their effort to serve purposes other than the quality of administration. But no one can quarrel with the central purpose of merit.

In any event, the first step in building a quality workforce is planning. The principal planner at all levels is the general operating supervisor, the individual we have been dubbing "the government manager." His is the task of envisaging what needs to be done; what kinds of workers will best serve those ends; and what details of quantity, time, and place are involved in building the necessary work-force.

We are dealing here with one of the most important areas of what may be termed "anticipatory management". The lower echelons of an organization are engaged in the chores of applying policy to individual cases, dealing with the public, answering inquiries, applying rules, and meeting today's needs. But any manager who spends most of his time on such matters is not performing as a manager. One of his prime reasons for being is to think and plan ahead. And no more important aspect of planning exists than that concerning personnel.

One element of this planning process has already been discussed at some length. This is the matter of designing jobs to meet the realities of the labor market, thereby contributing to both economical operations and social purposes. The need for this kind of deliberate job structuring would seem to be a foregone conclusion, but there are other considerations that must also be taken into account by the alert executive.

Past Is Prologue

The first such consideration, and perhaps the most elementary, is the fact that manpower estimation and projection need not be based on mere educated guesswork or experience-laden intuition. The single most influential factor bearing upon future manpower needs is past experience. The main ingredients of that experience are: the number of persons needed before; the loss rate and proportion of replacements needed; the lag between initial and full productivity of new appointees; training-time factors; and conditions of the labor market that might modify any of these circumstances in the future.

In some instances, nearly all the weight of prediction depends on extending such past experience into the future. Thus, if a manager knows that ten people could carry on a certain activity in the past, that he loses two a year on the average, and that it takes a half year for any appointee to become fully productive, he would be justified in concluding that his recruitment needs in that category for the year would be on the order of two and a half persons, or five in two years. This estimate would be without taking into account any expansion or contraction in the activity itself.

Being able to make such calculations is naturally dependent upon the adequacy of data about the past; and here is where the personnel office comes into the picture. It should routinely be gathering such information about accessions and turnover, so that each part of the public agency or jurisdiction can make intelligent analyses. But the analyses, to be tied in realistically with other factors in the situation, must be made by the operating offices themselves. When personnel offices do not provide this service, operating officials should find out why. They may well be of help in correcting the deficiency, whether the reason is disinclination, lack of imagination, or lack of resources.

In addition, it is incumbent upon each operating manager to take note of the total impact of this estimating process. If turnover in his segment of the public service is notably faster or slower than in other areas, he should know the reasons that account for this condition. If his activity seems to have more difficulty in attracting new blood, this should be a cause for concern. Losing people may not be bad per se—providing they are readily replaced. Consultation with personnel officials and other managers may offer clues to any peculiarities in the movements and replacements that characterize his organization. Whatever these peculiarities may be, they of course require study and treatment along a wider front than simply planning for recruitment and replacement. And they are the special responsibility of the manager himself, not someone else.

In short, much of what we tend to fear as hazardous "guestimating" is based on the solid experience with what went on before. All the manager needs is (1) authentic information about the past and (2) willingness to recognize the facts and act upon them as his own responsibility.

The Impact of Change

The more imponderable factor in projecting manpower needs is change in the program itself. Here again, the manager at any particular level of operation is the one who is in the best position to assess the significance of such changes.

Changes that may lead to contraction of the personnel force are usually the easiest to predict. They are likely to result from reductions in appropriations, curtailment of demand, or completion of special projects. In any case, the depth of change is often set by arbitrary or fairly clearly outlined parameters. What went into original estimates of manpower needs on such work is the main additional element that would have to be taken into account.

Prospective expansion is usually the most troublesome factor in attempting to make projections. If it is a quantitative expansion of something that has already existed, its effect on manpower needs may be mathematically computed. If the expansion involves a new and unprecedented program, the problem is much more difficult, and more careful attention must be given to the estimating. Usually the various occupational elements that compose the program can be isolated for individual analysis and some kind of composite contrived.

This is not the place to go into more detail, but two matters deserve emphasis: (1) the incidence of brand new programs is ordinarily very low in comparison with the relevance of past experience, so that there is more predictability in the average situation than is commonly supposed; and (2) the operating manager is the most authoritative source for the judgments, subjective or otherwise, as to the degree to which program changes will affect manpower needs.

A Common Job Language

If there were no system of occupational classification and definition, manpower estimating of any kind would be next to impossible. A sound job evaluation plan creates a common job language that permits relating past experience to future needs and compiling like components together, based on meaningful categorization of the work units that we call jobs. In most public jurisdictions such a job language is taken for granted, but the importance of its accuracy and adequacy for something more than pay equity is not always understood.

How can we say that we need only five persons in some category of personnel unless the past experience drawn upon relates to this same category? How can we analyze the impact of program changes unless we are able to break them down into realistic work categories? And how can we do either of these unless there is a standard means for categorizing work that is accepted and used by all parties?

One of the greatest handicaps of personnel systems that are based on artificial corps of people instead of on job analysis is the lack of facility for manpower planning.

Getting Candidates Interested

Attracting candidates to the service is definitely an area in which operating executives can participate intensively—with great profit to the operating programs, as well as serving good personnel policy on public-interest grounds.

Stressing the Work

One of the most critical levels of recruitment is that directed toward young people just out of high school, college, or graduate school. Time and again research studies have shown that the best students, especially those at the advanced level, are attracted more by the nature and challenge of work to be performed than by salary or fringe benefits. If this is so, then the most important single area to be exploited in recruiting the best minds would be the work itself. And the real experts on the inherent attractions of the work are those already engaged in it—the entire battery of operating supervisors.

It is impractical, of course, to enlist the participation of every supervisory executive in every recruitment campaign. However, several things can be done:

1. when the interest of engineers is being solicited, every effort can be made to have an engineer take the leadership in explaining the work incentives to engineering students and graduates, and similarly with every other occupational field (although there does not need to be a specialist for every sub-category of work);
2. different operating officials can be involved at dif-

ferent times, taking turns at selling the needs of the
total enterprise;

3. the technical knowledge of supervisors can be tapped
to ascertain what educational institutions and other
sources should be sought out; and

4. each participating executive can be expected to represent his agency or jurisdiction as a whole, not just
his particular sub-division.

Such activity should not be looked upon simply as sup-
plementing the work of the personnel office or civil service
commission. No matter how well-staffed and eager they
might be, such personnel units need the technical contributions of the operators to interpret the work to prospective candidates. As critical as the product of good recruitment is to operating success, these executives—far from
begrudging their time in such efforts—should accept this
participation as a natural part of their operating responsibilities. To do so may spell the difference between generating real attraction to an agency and having to be content
with mediocre candidates, who can always be counted on
to press their own cases. Superior people, who are interested
in what they are going to do, must be aggressively "sold"
on the worthwhileness of an enterprise before they will
apply for a job.

Not every jurisdiction may be able to corner the market of superior candidates, but each must make sure that it
gets a fair share. In the case of exceptional quality, the
competition nowadays is not so much between candidates
as between employers. Public employers in some areas
have an added disadvantage to overcome—an unfavorable
public image. All the more reason to stress the interesting
work to be done when conducting a recruiting campaign.

Some Pitfalls in Recruitment

We would be less than realistic if we ignored certain

obstacles to good, unfettered recruitment in the public service. The problems are not all solved through dedicated and aggressive selling—by operating officials or otherwise.

We have already taken note of some of the arbitrary restrictions inherited from bygone times that serve more as handicaps to recruitment than as reasoned public policy. Such restrictions include: residence requirements, veteran preference, and absurd educational or other standards. As long as these welfare-oriented or other conditions to public employment are not changed, they have to be honored by every line executive as well as by personnel officials.

But the real issue is the potentiality for change. Wherever government managers individually or collectively can make a good case for the ill effects of such policies, it is their obligation to make that case known to the responsible legislative bodies. Personnel officials may have to take the lead and coordinate such efforts, but they can make little headway unless operating leaders are willing to demonstrate that the quality of their work suffers because of arbitrary and inappropriate restrictions. The legislator will always ask: "Where are you hurting?" And only the operating managers can answer that.

Of course, the element of educational requirements is not ordinarily the product of legislation; this is usually within the province of administrative agencies to appraise and alter. Existing practices are often the result of a line of least resistance. Also, it may be the leadership in the very occupational field represented by the operating manager that has been responsible for the imposition of rigid, unverified educational credentials. Here again, the responsibility if not the initiative for improvement must be undertaken by those engaged in the field of work itself.

Another problem that has plagued recruiting efforts has been the inadequacy of institutional coverage. Only recently have many public jurisdictions gone out of their way to solicit interest and applications from minor, out-of-the-way schools as well as from prominent institutions, from associations of minority as well as majority groups. There is absolutely no evidence that the best candidates uniformly come from the most celebrated educational institutions. Today, the predominantly Negro colleges, the Indian Reservation schools, and the locales and societies of Spanish-speaking minorities must be sought out just as earnestly as traditional sources. The utility of this practice for a quality public service, as well as to insure genuinely equal opportunity, is already being demonstrated in many locations.

Methods of Attraction

There is hardly an up-to-date plan for positive development of interest in government employment that does not entail, or would not profit from, participation of the operating executives who are to supervise the workers being sought. Some of the best techniques build on what is going on in various government bureaus and programs: holding "open house" where an agency's functions lend themselves to public display (whether it be the local waterworks or a space science laboratory); maintaining dramatic and informative exhibits picturing government careers at conventions, fairs, and similar assemblages; disseminating feature articles to the public press and periodicals about the work of government departments; and seizing upon every opportunity to engage in "institutional advertising" through radio, television, and other media in order to develop a public awareness of specific government activities, their achievements, and the ways in which civil servants contribute to their success. Such techniques cannot ordinarily be worked out by the personnel people, at least not alone; they demand the program know-how of the operating managers in government.

In addition, much profitable recruitment depends on a

policy of continuing constructive relationships, not only with the general public, but also with those special publics that are likely to be the principal sources for future candidates. Nothing quite takes the place of long-term favorable relationships with college placement officers, heads of college academic departments, technical journal editors, labor leaders, and other influential professional and technical men. Obviously, the government people in the best position to cultivate and maintain such relationships are the program executives in charge of the various activities for which prospects are being recruited.

To summarize, the attraction of enough of the best candidates to a particular jurisdiction is much more than a process of aggressive campaigning. It is the product of long-standing, painstaking cultivation of sources and the development of an institutional image that pays off when specific efforts at recruitment are undertaken. The key actor in this drama is the government manager, who stands to profit from sound, positive recruitment policies.

Contributing to Competition

The average government manager may not find it difficult to accept his role in basic recruitment, but he asks: "What about that examination system? That's something else again." And he may be right. If so, it is his fault or the fault of his personnel officer, or both; for he has a vital role in the entire fabric of the competitive process through objective examination. The process is not—or at least it should not be—something extraneous to the operating concerns of government program offices.

At least two aspects of this subject deserve elaboration: the direct involvement of supervisory officials in the design and conduct of competitive examinations; and the influence they can bring to find ways of measuring attributes not previously evaluated.

Design and Conduct of Examinations

There is no perfect method for predicting how well people are going to work out on a job, but there are vast differences between methods as to their *relative* validity.

Most public service examinations consist of several elements or devices designed to gauge the candidate's background, knowledge, and/or skill. In various combinations, we find such specific parts as: systematic analyses of previous employment history and educational preparation; written tests; oral tests; performance tests; and investigation or inquiry among previous employers or teachers. Some examinations may contain several of these devices. The only device that is occasionally relied on as the sole method of examination is the first one—analysis of employment and educational history. With reference to novices in any field, looking to previous employment records is not very productive; accordingly more reliance is put on written tests in filling junior positions than for more senior posts.

Supervisors do not ordinarily concern themselves with the methodology of examining typists, stenographers, clerks, and machine operators; they know that performance and aptitude testing for such occupations has been pretty well standardized. Although improvements are still needed—and continue to be made from time to time—supervisors are content to leave these developments to the personnel specialists.

The operator's main concern is usually with the methods for evaluating candidates for occupations that form the journeyman backbone of his organization. These may be economists, police officers, computer operators, electric linemen, social welfare workers, tax analysts, accountants, or any of a number of professional or technical specialists that take the major actions in carrying on a public program. In such areas the operator not only has a legitimate interest but may also have the subject-matter information the application of which could spell the difference between a mediocre measuring instrument and a realistic, useful one.

Among the ways in which this specialized knowledge may be brought to bear on the examination process are these:

1. Panels of operating executives may outline the criteria that form the basis of a systematic appraisal format for evaluating previous experience and education.
2. They may contribute draft questions or "test items," particularly when the test covers subject-matter knowledge.
3. They may cooperate in studies of the comparative performance of employees on tests and on the job, so as to get a line on the degree to which the tests actually measure what they purport to measure.
4. They may sit on committees of interviewers in oral examinations and record their estimates of how candidates stack up in respect to qualities measurable by this process.
5. They may meet with personnel officials from time to time to discuss any or all aspects of the examining system, constantly seeking improvements and reporting experiences that will facilitate such improvement.

Over the years the use of written tests of subject-matter knowledge has declined in favor of aptitude testing—that is, testing for certain natural capacities (verbal, mathematical, reasoning, and so forth), since these in various combinations can be related to a wide variety of occupations. The sheer number of vocational specializations that have developed in modern times has made separate knowledge or achievement tests burdensome and impractical.

Moreover, aptitude testing has lent itself more readily to gauging general abilities that are useful in many occupations across the board—especially such managerial ones as administrative analyst, budget examiner, personnel specialist, purchasing officer, and other widely-distributed administrative specialties.

The manner in which operators can contribute to designing test questions on general aptitude tests may not be as clear as for achievement tests, but the special parts of such tests do require the services of those with specialized skills. Thus, items on mathematics are supplied by accountants, statisticians, engineers, and mathematicians; items on verbal facility are supplied by editors, writers, lawyers, and various kinds of analysts; and so on.

Two kinds of executives will not be called upon to participate in the development and conduct of examinations: those who demonstrate by their cavalier handling of personnel matters that they have neither the integrity nor intellectual stamina to contribute much; and those administrative wallflowers who have no ideas or insights to contribute. The official who is enthusiastic about his program, knows what he needs in the way of human competence, takes the time and trouble to study his situation and that of his fellow managers, and is articulate about his ideals and his problems in the selection process will almost invariably be called upon to engage himself actively in competitive examining in the ways enumerated.

Measuring the Intangibles

Not many would disagree that we have failed to do very much systematically about some of the factors that are most critical to the process of selection of people for employment. We have concentrated on raw knowledge and abstract skill, but we know that failures and successes often have to do with more elusive qualities—such as creativity, courage, and commitment to the cause. Personnel experts have not given the need for these considerations the attention and leadership it deserves. There is room for more active participation by all who supervise the efforts of others to help devise ways of predicting whether candidates are worth the risk. Refined evaluations may seem beyond realization, but not even rough categorization has been achieved.

Most executives are appreciative of the significant difference that a creative person on the staff can make. They know how comforting it is to see a display of intellectual courage. Above all, they sense more than anyone else the enormous influence on performance of genuine interest, zeal, and dedication to a public mission. To such executives these charactertistics are the essence of merit; and they may well wonder whether some of the traditional criteria that sail under the banner of merit can really be as important.

Attacks on Testing. Such executives are tempted therefore to fall prey to the undiscriminating and mindless attacks on testing that have come from several quarters. Some of these attacks are born of lack of understanding, and some are due to a deliberate plot to undermine the whole concept that excellence shall be rewarded. Several writers have wrongfully censured the entire field of testing, basing their evidence on the one narrow area of "personality testing", which has never been recognized as a valid methodology by reputable measurement psychologists. Improvements are always needed; but, by and large, the testing of intelligence, aptitude, and achievement has served useful purposes exceedingly well and has really been the backbone of policies that insure elimination of extraneous, prejudicial factors in the selection process.

If the test experts deserve a prod, it is not because they have failed to hone their instruments so much as they have failed to press their researches more extensively into new

69

areas. The testing of aptitudes is very well done, but the gauging of creativity is correspondingly neglected. True, it is a much more intangible quality to define, and therefore to assess, than abilities that may be estimated by probes into knowledge of information or into skills in manipulating facts or concepts. Such attributes as courage and commitment are even more elusive.

But this is all the more reason for investing adequate resources in these more difficult areas. If as much time and investigation had been spent in studying creativity as has been squandered in analyzing "personality," we would be much farther down the road to perfecting selection processes. Personality is not the important factor that some have assumed; wide variations in personality characteristics can sustain equal levels of performance. The critical differentiating factors in success, besides the elementary considerations of ability that are already adequately probed, are the three "Cs": creativity, courage, and commitment.

The Manager Can Help. The government manager may feel somewhat helpless in this situation, but he should not be. He usually has access to the larger resources that may be drawn upon for measurement research. His direct concern with the quality of personnel in his operation gives his voice authority. He is often in a position to divert resources from less important projects to more important ones. The government establishments are still numerous that spend more money on inventorying, maintaining control over, and repairing typewriters or other equipment than on personnel selection processes. There seems to have been little difficulty in many jurisdictions in dredging up the large sums needed to purchase or rent computers. The same or lesser amounts spent on personnel assessment studies would result in more pay-off in the long run.

Those who assault testing in general offer no substitute for the sorting and winnowing that are unavoidable in all large employment situations. Those who are genuinely concerned about excellence, in seeing to it that it is effectively identified and used, can best serve the cause of a quality public service by supporting both the intelligent use of existing personnel measurement instruments and the expansion of knowledge to develop new methods.

Mobility and Promotion

For convenience in dealing with the special problems of selection from among applicants from outside the organization, we have so far concentrated on that aspect of filling positions. But selection from within is just as important and just as complicated. If we total all the occasions when positions are filled with new faces, far more will result from movement of personnel within the organization than from new accessions from outside. Internal mobility is thus greater in magnitude.

Of basic importance also is the fact that the information about persons already in the organization is vastly more detailed and certain than that obtainable about outside applicants. This requires some fundamental differences in methodology, principally that more reliance can be placed on reports of past performance and estimates of future potential of those already employed than is the case with outsiders. This is why written tests are more appropriate for outsiders than insiders; they are in effect substitutes for direct observation on the job.

This is not to say that written tests need never be used on selections from within. There are instances, as when large numbers of police patrolmen are aspirants to smaller numbers of higher ranks, where written tests of program knowledge or aptitude are needed to supplement other methods. In such cases, the necessity of reducing the number of final competitors to manageable proportions requires more refined categorization than is likely to be provided by performance criteria alone.

Balance of Practice

One of the most common complaints of operating managers is that the "system" does not permit them to make independent determinations in selecting employees for transfer or promotion on the basis of their personal knowledge of the merits of the respective candidates. There are several flaws to the seeming plausibility of this reasoning: (1) no one supervisor can possibly know the merits of potential candidates from other parts of the organization, or even whether there are any; (2) managers are not always in a position to see all angles of the behavior and competence of their own subordinates, whose activities often have an impact not only as supervisors themselves but also in their relations with other units of the enterprise; (3) career opportunities are meaningless unless they extend to as wide a field as feasible, so that managers must not expect to confine their determinations to their own respective segments of the total organization; and (4) executives who attempt to operate in isolation are open to the charge of favoritism and "playing God" with the fortunes of individual workers.

Overcoming Provinciality. An organization-wide instead of a provincial point of view would suggest that each supervisory manager must consider himself as representing the interests of the entire activity, not merely his own part of it. This may be an entire public jurisdiction, or in the very largest jurisdictions an entire department.

It is possible that some occupations will be so concentrated in one agency or sub-division of a jurisdiction that effective competition for promotion or lateral movement can be achieved within that organization alone. But most occupations are scattered throughout at least several departments; and some—like the managerial support fields of accounting, budgeting, administrative analysis, personnel work, computer programming and operation, and so forth —exist in some measure in almost every department. In these cases, nothing less than jurisdiction-wide competition will serve the twin objectives of: (1) seeing to it that management assigns the best talent available from anywhere in the organization to the best jobs; and (2) providing the widest opportunity to employees to be considered for vacancies for which they are qualified, no matter where they may occur. The accident of distribution of jobs and of turnover should not determine who gets promoted. When this is the case, some able people are stuck in dead-end units, while others no more able, or even less able, may enjoy extraordinarily rapid promotion.

Upholding Organization-Wide Interests. To achieve a balance in opportunity both for management and for employees requires a promotion policy based on the magnitude, concentration, and dynamism in each broad occupational category. Does this mean that individual supervisors must be denied freedom of choice in their own domains? It most certainly does, and for good reason. It is simply a matter of the good of the entire organization over what may appear to be the immediate welfare of a particular unit and its employees. Actually, of course, what is good for the entire organization is good for that unit. Choices that may seem best in the myopic view of one manager, focusing on his own narrow bailiwick, are not necessarily the best when a wider field of possibilities is taken into account.

Reference was made earlier to the necessity for managers to be judges and not just advocates; and this is one of the areas in which that aphorism has application. The manager who stands on his presumed "right" to ignore the interests of the rest of the enterprise is not much of a manager. His unit and portion of the total mission is not his private preserve to exploit as he pleases. Unfortunately, the time-worn concept of authority commensurate with responsibility has been taken by some to mean irresponsibility. Conformance with a sensible promotion policy is one of the obligations that suffers when this attitude is taken.

In short, managers who accept their full share of personnel management responsibility are prepared to appoint employees whom they do not know over some they do know, based on objective evaluations of their relative worth (a process in which all managers may participate) and to lose employees whom they value very highly to other parts of the jurisdiction. They understand that this means that the best jobs everywhere really get the best people from anywhere, without regard to the accident of where the jobs and the people happen to be located.

This philosophy places a lot of faith in the processes by which the "best" are singled out. No one pretends that anyone has invented the perfect promotional selection device, but as long as operating managers collectively have a large role in developing and operating selection devices, they cannot object that they are remote from reality.

Resisting Seniority

There is one selection policy, however, that is inherently so antithetical to the merit concept that it deserves special comment. One of the most unfortunate tendencies of American unionism has been the fostering of the idea that the only way to prevent favoritism and abuse of power is to advance employees purely on the basis of seniority. Usually this policy has meant seniority in a particular work unit, rather than total length of experience. It is one of the most insidious sappers of incentive for superior performance and the most vicious denials of the merit idea that exists.

One need only observe those organizations that have been traditionally seniority-ridden—both public and private—to see the contrast with those in which excellence ranks higher than durability. Lack-lustre operations, absence of creativity and responsiveness to change, avoidance of responsibility, disdain for the client and other members of the public—these are the earmarks of the organization that has succumbed to seniority as a guiding principle. The approach is utterly the opposite of the competition, drive, and imagination that have explained so much of America's high productivity.

Here is where administrators need to make their stand. They should resist at all costs the encroachment of seniority on their latitude, or far more important, on the quality of their organization's performance. Their own prerogatives are best protected by wholehearted participation in promotion and mobility policies founded on merit, even when they contain some elements, as they often must, of subjective judgment (in which they as managers usually share). Even if performance evaluation systems are faulty and require constant repair, even if tests need improvement, even if supervisory judgments are fallible, they are far superior to the dead hand of mere staying-power as an automatic guide to employee progress.

It is the duty of every thinking government executive to stand fast against the erosion of quality that is the inevitable consequence of reliance on the easy road of seniority. Indefensible personal favoritism, inadequate attention to sound merit methods, narrow provincial points of view —are reprehensible enough and must be exorcised to the fullest. But no practice is more deleterious to organizational health and productivity in the long run than those over-simplified promotion practices that result in little more than the progressive advancement of mediocrity.

Facing Up to Release

Implicit in what has been said about promotion and transfer policy is the assumption that mobility of personnel within a government department or jurisdiction is a worthwhile condition. The reasons behind this assumption are threefold:

1. constructive mobility helps broaden the perspectives of employees by giving them new responsibilities and new challenges from time to time;
2. different parts of the organization are energized by introducing "new blood" and fresh points of view;
3. using the entire organization as a placement ground maintains more meaningful career development opportunities for rank and file as well as key workers, a condition that redounds to the benefit of both the mission and its agents.

Even without a deliberate policy in that direction, mobility seems to be the order of the day. The inexorable impact of technological and sociological change sees to that. Gone are the days when the average technical or professional worker found the full scope of his career within one enterprise in one location; even clerical employees experience much more diversity in their careers than ever before.

However, for mobility to avoid too much dependence on the vicissitudes of fortune, it must be planned and purposeful. This means that individual units cannot operate in isolation from the total activity. It also means that there is no room for a protective attitude on the part of supervisors with reference to their subordinates. Employees working for them are not their property; they are not to be hoarded against outside "depredations"—which are really opportunities.

Managers who take the long view are not afraid of losing their staffs. They know that this experience is not only good for the enterprise as a whole, but that it improves their own lot in at least two ways: (1) replacements are more likely to be people of breadth and sophistication because of their diversity of experiences; and (2) their units will gain a reputation for being places of genuine opportunity, which is attractive to ambitious and high-caliber prospects. The supervisory official who interposes objections to the release of one of his best workers is only punishing himself in the long run—he succeeds in retaining a resentful employee, and when he does lose him he finds it difficult to replace him because the unit has the reputation of being a "dead-end" shop.

The objection may well be raised that this view is very costly in terms of breaking-in time and maintaining continuity. True, but the modern manager must discipline himself to accept this as a fact of organizational existence. Such costs are seldom as expensive as husbanding cadres of employees who are provincial in outlook, wanting in creativity, and short on the kind of imaginative service that is the product of diversity and perspective in experience.

Of equal importance to facilitating release of employees for transfer and promotion is releasing the best of them for purposes of formal training. More is to be said in the next chapter concerning the significance and forms of employee training. At this point we are stressing the importance of making it easy for the better workers to be relieved of their formal duties to take advantage of training opportunities that deepen their insights, sharpen their skills, and broaden their horizons. Determining who shall engage in an off-the-job training exercise is all too often translated into: "Who can be spared?" This is self-defeating: it not only denies opportunities to those who deserve them most; it also denies the organization the performance of employees who are likely to benefit most from educational experiences, who are in the best position to provide return value to the organization.

77

It takes a good deal of supervisory self-discipline to look upon the loss of a good worker, either temporarily for training or permanently for transfer, as a positive good. To be able to do so is one of the tests of mature, managerial judgment. The whining official who panics at the thought of releasing a reliable employee at a critical juncture had better not continue with the trying task of supervision and management. In his type of vision, the myopia induced by the trees of immediate, localized advantage completely obscures the grander forest of over-all organizational effectiveness.

Sharing in Selection

Aside from the repudiated method of seniority, the measures used to determine the best candidates—whether for initial appointment or for promotion—are:

- comparison of previous education and experience;
- comparison of performance within the organization;
- objective testing of skills and aptitudes; and
- trial on the job.

The government manager has a role in all of these, but particularly in points two and four, so far as selections from within the organization are concerned.

Another way of looking at the selection process is this: it is a means of determining who gets appointed, singling out who has access to training, appraising the effectiveness of performance, predicting human potential, and deciding who gets promoted. These various steps come into play in various combinations in influencing the decisions that govern entry and mobility of personnel in any organization. Competition, whether for initial entry or advancement, involves an infinite variety of ways in which any or all of these elements are brought to bear on a personnel decision.

Challenges to Selection Power. Traditionally, it has

been the habit of writers and administrators to stress that such selection decisions are the prerogative of the line executive. This is true when we speak of the executive function; but this does not mean that each individual executive is privileged to act independently. Furthermore, as employee organizations or unions in the public service have become more vocal, there has been increasing resistance to unchecked selection power on the part of individual supervisory officials.

We have already noted the necessity for all executives to subordinate their parochial interests to those of the whole organization. Most personnel systems, nevertheless, are built on the principle that the final word in placing an individual in a job is that of the executive in charge. Up to a point this makes sense. When all the control requisites and the criteria based on merit have been met, when all candidates are approximately equal in measuring up to the standards of quality called for, when the only other considerations that could influence the final choice are intangibles not gauged by the system, then it seems perfectly reasonable that the government manager should have the latitude in selecting from among the limited number of candidates who comprise the premium group. The question is whether this latitude might not be too parochial to permit full compliance with objectivity.

Employee suspicions that this final selection power of the manager is not always fair or in the best interests of the organization are common in most government jurisdictions. Such suspicions, well-founded or not, constitute the motivation for escape into arbitrary methods, such as seniority. Any fair-minded person would agree that the great majority of executives make such decisions with the utmost regard for both equity and the welfare of the enterprise. And this writer, if he had his choice, would still opt for unbridled executive selection authority in comparison with the mechanistic and hopeless seniority method.

But there is an additional dimension to the issue: in all situations is any one executive really in possession of the information and understanding necessary to make a wise selection? For routine operations that have little contact with persons or units outside the particular activity, and for appointments or promotions where the field from which candidates are drawn is adequately broad, where all truly qualified and eligible individuals have a fair chance, and where the final decision is not especially difficult or critical, there is little reason to challenge management's final selection authority. The remedy for irresponsible or faulty decisions in these cases should not be to change the system but to change the offending official.

However, there are situations where a given manager may not be best equipped to make the critical judgment, even though he is wise and judicious and in charge of the activity that is to be manned. Examples of such situations are: filling positions which are brand new to the enterprise and for which there has been no internal precedent or experience; selecting persons for jobs which have extensive negotiation or other relationships with other parts of the organization, outside clients, or other branches or levels of government; filling key positions which are of a critical nature as to level, visibility, and impact on the public good; and estimating the future potential of an employee. It is in such cases that reliance on final selection by some single executive may not be good enough to insure the most complete and genuine conformance with the spirit of the merit system—not because the manager is unwilling or does not try to do the right thing, but because he may be unable to do so or unable to demonstrate to all concerned the correctness of his action.

Shared Power. What, then, might be done? The executive involved need not be stripped of all power in the process; instead, common sense would suggest that he be bolstered—which leads us to the conclusion that there is safety in numbers. Such an instance may well be the most apt example of the truth of the old adage that several heads are better than one.

In other words, final selection in these most difficult cases could be left to a panel or committee, where each member has a special reason for serving. One member should definitely be the supervisory manager in whose division the prospective appointee is expected to work. Another might be a representative of clientele groups within and outside the organization which will be dealing most intimately with the successful candidate. Some members might be former supervisors of the various candidates. Still another might be an expert—preferably from within the organization—in the occupational field for which the selection is being made. Occasionally, in highly specialized and professionalized work, a representative of the employee group most involved might also be included.

The details of making up such a panel, and identifying the instances when it is to be used, must be left to each occasion and purpose. Imaginative administration is capable of working out the machinery and the code of practices. The important point is that the final selection would be by multiple judgment, instead of being invariably and irrevocably by individual judgment. Adoption of such an approach would be an innovation in most public —and private—bureaucracies. While it may appear to do violence to that sacrosanct fetish that the manager must always have the final choice, it would not really deprive him of weighty influence, it would apply to only specified kinds of situations, and it would go far to insure the organization of wise and defensible choices in its most critical selections.

When all is said and done, the opportunities and obligations of the government manager to maintain the most effective human resources for his enterprise are both numerous and substantial. His power over advance planning, his influence on and participation in recruitment, his necessary role in fostering realistic competition, his inducement of sound mobility practices, and his final selection authority or sharing in selection—are all personnel activities of the most critical order. The fact that in so many of these processes the manager must see beyond the confines of his own territory and must share power is no derogation of his influence or authority. We take for granted that he must operate with full regard for the public interest. His judgments about people are part of fulfilling that obligation.

To direct an operation in conformance with all, not just part, of what is expected is not simply management under constraint, it is the utmost of responsibility. The public executive's manpower determinations are among his most difficult and sensitive, but also his most rewarding. They occupy a major share, sometimes a preponderance, of his time. They comprise the essence of what government managers are for.

5

Training

THERE ARE few managers today who fail to appreciate or use formal training as a major resource in the development of their staffs. Some of their predecessors were not so understanding—or so venturesome. It has been only a few decades since government executives had to be prodded or cajoled into allowing their employees to take part in educational programs designed to strengthen their performance. The reasons for this reluctance were complex; among them, undoubtedly, was a sense of insecurity on the part of these executives, an unarticulated (even to themselves) fear that acknowledging a training need was somehow an exposure of their own failures.

Those more gifted and farsighted public administrators (beginning in the 1930s) who dared to surmount this feeling, who recognized that a variety of methodologies in addition to experience contribute to staff development and improvement, broke the ice. The results were dramatic. Their daring had a rippling effect throughout the public service. Never in the history of public administration has there been such rapid and extensive acceptance of a novel approach: the recognition of the good that comes from investing in systematic, purposeful in-service training. Training has now become fashionable. If anything, today's problems center on how to be more discriminating in the use of training, how to avoid charlatanism and poorly organized programs, and how to use new methods and forms, rather than on generation of acceptance.

Government's Needs

Little thought is necessary to discern how foolish and short-sighted it was of so many top civil servants of yesteryear to have passed up opportunities to permit their subordinates to participate in training (or to participate themselves); or to have failed to see the need to initiate and help organize training programs. The incredible notions that merit-system appointees were already trained, and that if they did not perform well it was the fault of the selection process, were not tenable very long.

Government managers soon bowed to such realities of a complex, modern public service as the following:

1. Many occupations are unique to the public service, with no counterparts for which there is a ready-made labor supply in the general market and for which educational institutions automatically turn out suitable candidates.

2. With the advance of technology, occupations evolve continuously, requiring that previously well-prepared incumbents keep abreast of developments in their specialties.

3. Public programs are changing frequently and substantially, introducing the necessity for periodic new "tooling up" of the staff.

4. People are being recruited more and more for broad categories of work instead of specific niches, thus requiring orientation in each activity in which individual jobs are located.

5. Tighter labor markets are forcing more attention to preparing employees for advancement beyond an entry level and to insuring career opportunities.

In addition, it was penetrating the consciousness of many administrators that training of some kind was taking place in every work situation; the issue was simply whether it was to be planned or haphazard, effective or inefficient. They were becoming aware that there were real differences between organizations in such behavioral features as courtesy and attitude of employees toward the public, their knowledge about the mission and functions of the enterprise, and their skill and speed in performing a service. It became increasingly evident that one of the most revealing explanations for such differences was to be found in an organization's training policies and practices.

In the light of these almost self-evident facts it is anachronistic to come upon a supervisor today who fears the loss of subordinates if he lets them be trained for better things. Such resistance to release of promising employees for training boomerangs on the resisting executive. He not only loses the chance to develop a reputation for quality performance of his staff, he also loses the advantage of easy replacement that accrues to an outfit with a reputation for upward mobility.

The imposing demands made on public services nowadays—from the international realm to the urban jurisdiction—are too insistent and too overwhelming to permit static bureaucracies. Every civil servant needs exposure to new ideas—even controversy—if he is to measure up to the requirements of the job; the rapidity and magnitude of change makes this all the more compelling.

Much has been said about man's need for self-renewal.

John W. Gardner, with great discernment, has pointed out the tendency for people to become complacent and has urged the exploitation of every means to induce self-appraisal and revitalization. He has observed, as have others, that it is the tendency of most occupations, especially the professions, to become set in their ways and to resist change. When change is the most characteristic feature of our civilization, this rigidity is not only foolhardy, it is downright dangerous.

Of all places where these truths need emphasis, it is in the public service. Its position at the hub of human activity, its monitoring of traffic in human affairs, its power to influence public purpose, to induce order and meaning and beauty in human relationships, make especially vital a spirit of adaptation and self-renewal among its offices and its agents. The inescapable fact is that if government fails in modern civilization, then civilization fails.

Not the only, but certainly one of the most important, forces in creating an environment of adaptability and renewal is purposeful, systematic education. Its form and techniques are many and varied, and its role in the workaday world is not yet fully defined. But we do know this much: continuing education is a part of the work itself. It is as much a responsibility as collecting a tax, paving a street, signing a treaty, or finding a cure for cancer. It is, in fact, fundamental to all of these. For many types of work the day is not far off when a quarter or more of working time (over a span of years) will be spent in training. This point has already been reached in some fields. Training is indeed a facet of the job.

Training for What? and How?

An exhaustive treatment of the ends and forms of inservice training is left to more specialized works; here it should suffice to outline briefly the principle categories of content and method, simply for the purpose of clarifying the subject under discussion.

Scope

If we accept the unchallengeable thesis that there are few instances where employees are fully prepared for the specific tasks they are assigned, if we accept the inevitability of change in program content and therefore job content, if we accept the need to keep up with developments in the technology of an occupation, then it is easy to see that formal devices for sharpening and directing performance are essential to all modern enterprise. Among them are the following principal kinds of training:

1. Orientation—the preparation and indoctrination of new employees in the objectives, policies, organization, and methods of operation of the activity, as well as in the specific duties and requirements of the jobs which they are entering.
2. Improving Performance—the systematic inculcation of improved skills, new insights, and new information, so as to induce the highest quality performance of employees in their existing jobs.
3. Extension of Employee Capacity
    - to take on new or higher responsibilities;
    - to learn how to supervise other employees effectively;
    - to build a reservoir of talent for ultimate top leadership

This is a very sketchy list, but almost any kind of training that can be envisaged can be fitted under it. Note that every one of these categories is central to the daily operating effectiveness of the organization; each is clearly of prime concern to every alert operating manager.

Methods

Methods of training are, of course, of even wider variety. The most important single educational influence is the job itself—about which we shall have more to say later. The point to be emphasized here is that the job is still an under-used, little understood factor and that its exploitation is almost wholly within the province of program supervisors and managers. Other and more recognizable methods are: planned reading; conference and discussion groups; formal classes, which embrace many approaches, including lectures, task forces, case studies, role playing, and the like; and ready-made formal courses obtained from full-time educational institutions.

Administration

In the planning, promotion, management, and evaluation of all these forms and methods of training, modern personnel offices or other special training establishments usually supply support through a staff of one or more training experts. Although these specialists may be drawn from a number of fields, they usually have one thing in common: they tend to be practitioners in educational organization or methodology. Now, this is neither good nor bad per se; there are top performers and mediocre ones in this as in any other field of endeavor. The point is that such specialists work best as facilitators and coordinators; they are not necessarily expert in the subject matter of the training itself—although over periods of time many become so. Subject content, acquaintance with specialists outside the organization, and knowledge of program goals and problems are more likely to be found in the minds of the government program managers whose employees are the objects of training. The "training man" is a definite asset to have on hand, but he cannot develop or run a training program on his own; he can do it only with and through the supervisors themselves.

The Manager's Role

Once again, then, we come to the important place occupied by the government executive in personnel administration, in this case in what is perhaps its most constructive aspect—training. There is hardly a facet of the training process in which his role is not significant; in many it is crucial.

Diagnosing Needs

Who else is in a better position to determine what the deficiencies or growth needs of employees are? Others, such as the training experts or administrators at the very apex, may sense special needs when new program directions or philosophy are being promoted or when public clientele demands call for staff improvement. Likewise, the continuous need to prepare people for broader or different responsibilities may not always be perceived by individual program managers as readily as by those at more Olympian vantage points. However, for the day-to-day operations that are served by good orientation and skill improvement, few can match the manager-in-charge for knowledge of what the shortcomings or challenges are and of what must be stressed to overcome them.

Thus, analysis of training needs begins with the supervisory manager. Not only is it his obligation to respond to the initiatives of others, he must be sufficiently observant and resourceful to conduct or to suggest training activities on his own.

Helping Organize

By the same token, the manager is the most important

single resource in giving life to a training idea. Technical help he may well need—in sharpening his aims, selecting the most effective methods, and appraising the educational programs available on the market; but his active participation in the design and operation of a training program is a necessity. At a minimum, he must be consulted at every step along the way; and he must accept this as a normal responsibility, not an encroachment on his time.

There may, of course, be instances where he handles the entire operation himself. This may be true where the subject matter is technical or specialized, or where the goals are limited to his in-house functions and involvement of others is either unnecessary or superfluous. In any event, he must be deeply involved in planning, defining purposes, selecting methods, soliciting instructors, operating the program, and evaluating the results of any training affecting employees under his direction.

Releasing Workers

Mention has been made in other connections of the critical importance of a liberal release policy that permits employees to participate in needed training. The key to implementation of such a policy is the cooperation of government managers up and down the line. Where the manager himself has perceived the need for the training or has at least participated in its design, it is hard to imagine any difficulty in this regard.

Problems are more likely in those programs which originate elsewhere, such as at higher levels of management. The manager may need to be reminded of the importance to the organization as a whole (as well as to his own operation) of assigning to training not simply those employees who can be "spared" but those who can make the most of the opportunity, from whom the organization can expect the greatest gains. Any danger of losing employees to other jobs as the result of exposing them to training is easily offset by the gain to the organization as a whole and, even in the narrow sense, by the greater attractiveness of the manager's own shop for future replacements. If a manager's unwillingness to assign competent workers to a training effort is based on his doubts about the utility of that effort, his best procedure is to question the program directly, not further contribute to its ineffectiveness by assigning second-rate people as participants.

Stimulating the Will To Learn

In spite of all the talk about rebelliousness and defiance of today's employees, very few of them—especially in the public service—fail to take note of and be influenced by the opinions and attitudes of their superior officers. If the attitude toward training is disparaging or disdainful, motivation to learn is hardly fostered. If workers are dispatched to participate in a training program about which they have heard their supervisors express doubts or make aspersive "cracks", they are stymied from the start. More important, their participation will almost surely be a waste of time. In short, negative supervisory expectations are only too likely to be fulfilled.

On the other hand, if they hear from their leaders repeated expressions of faith in the educational process, avowals of desire to see improved performance therefrom, and determination to use every educational advantage to advance the cause of the government program, the chances are that they will be stimulated to make the most of all training opportunities. Motivation to learn is invariably based on positive, not negative, incentives.

To repeat, if any government manager has genuine doubts about the efficacy of any particular training program, he should deal with the matter forthrightly by raising questions with those in charge. If he is right and has evidence to support his doubts, his case is more likely than not to have an impact. Merely grumbling to the unwitting participants serves no constructive purpose and only contributes to a waste of government time and funds.

Serving as Instructors

Another way in which managers take part in in-service training is to serve as instructors or discussion leaders in formal group sessions. Training specialists often have difficulty in finding qualified persons to serve as faculty in the courses that they organize. There is nothing like the busy executive who "knows his stuff" to serve in this capacity. When called upon, he should so manage his time that he can give the assignment the quality attention that it deserves. In fact, he should volunteer when he knows that his expertise is needed.

When a manager has a genuine concern for the development of the staff, he should relish the opportunity to impart his knowledge and wisdom. The managing role is very much a teaching role. In fact, some would contend that it is entirely a teaching role. This does not mean that all good teachers make good managers; but it does mean that all managers had better be good teachers! If the manager shrinks from the role of instructor, there is good reason to question his general qualifications as a manager.

Bringing in Resource People

Especially when we are dealing with training in substantive subjects with which government programs are concerned, the supervisory manager in charge is usually a fountainhead of information about specialists throughout the country who excel in research, practice, or knowledge in his particular field. If he is not acquainted or in touch with his counterparts elsewhere, the question may again be raised about his qualifications for the job he holds. But, on the assumption that he is qualified and does have such contacts, he probably is the most important single source of advice on resource people to be drawn into training ventures in his area of expertise. Whoever is organizing the training program will usually welcome the ideas and suggestions of the knowledgeable executive who can identify leaders whose names and contributions will lend prestige and quality to the training undertaken.

Evaluation

Needless to say, every manager has a responsibility to participate in the evaluation of any training that has a significant impact on his employees. Training evaluation is at best an elusive and difficult process. Without the participation of operating supervisors it may well become an empty and useless process.

The wisdom and practical observations of government managers are essential to any evaluation worthy of the name. But to give effect to this truism means calling upon the supervisor's time. Constructing questionnaires, interviewing employees or others, constructing appraisal techniques, are examples of those processes in which such executives may properly be called upon to apply their skill and their insight. Indeed, alert managers should insist on participating in this phase of training; for it is here that the shaping of future training emphases and directions takes place; and it is here that the impact on the performance of employees in their programs may be most influential.

Attendance at Professional Meetings

One area of administrative practice, not commonly thought of as relating to training but which may have enormous educational impact, is the matter of encouraging employees to participate in outside professional activities. One of the most telling educational experiences an employee can have is exposure to the thinking and work of his colleagues outside his own organization. This may be gained in part by participation in meetings and conventions of the professional groups with which his function is most closely related.

Traditionally it has been the attitude of appropriating bodies—city councils, state legislatures, and Congressional committees—that reimbursement for travel and other expenses for attendance at professional meetings is a frill, an extra-curricular indulgence that might be exploited more as a reward for faithful service than as a deliberate training device. This attitude has accounted, in part, for the efforts of administrative officials to keep such expenditure and participation in check—lest too many employees indulge in happy holidays away from the job at rollicking conventions.

That some such conventions have indeed become too socially-oriented should not detract from the fact that the overwhelming bulk of such meetings are serious affairs where all participants gain tremendously from exchanges of views and experiences. A judicious and liberal use of attendance at professional meetings as a conscious training opportunity, that might not otherwise be available to his employees, should be part of the development arsenal of every progressive government executive.

The pay-off is often greater per unit of time and dollar expended than from more deliberately planned training. The dignity and freedom thus accorded the professional man may pay substantial dividends. He is not singled out as having a particular learning need such as might be implied by his selection to participate in a formal training course. Instead, he is given the opportunity to rub shoulders and exchange views with colleagues from all over the country, even all over the world. This is an experience that may be infinitely more rewarding and satisfying. He may well return to his job with a zest and enthusiasm that is far more valuable than the hours he missed from his post of duty.

Using the Job

We have already explored the critical role of the job itself as a facet of the administrative process; but it has an equally significant role as an educational influence; indeed, it may be *the* single most significant educational influence. This statement is made not to downgrade formal training efforts, but to emphasize the fact that the most formidable training instrument may be right under the supervisor's nose. It is an instrument totally unencumbered by considerations of organizing formal classes, release from duty time, and all the other atttributes we think of as constituting training.

By using the job itself, we refer to planned and deliberate assignments designed to enlarge an employee's knowledge and experience, rotation among different jobs to introduce a change of pace and atmosphere, trial assignments or delegations to give an employee a realistic measure of his prowess, and opportunities to develop improvements in work processes or practices. All such steps are within the jurisdiction of every supervisory manager—with few or no restraints. Also, substituting different employees in supervisory slots during absences of their superiors is another practice that provides training opportunities, chances to evaluate relative performance, and also practical tests of merit and prospective promotability.

The possibilities inherent in using the job as an educational venture are almost as extensive as the variety of jobs themselves. When such use of assignments is purposeful and not haphazard, its value is scarcely matched by any other technique; its virtue is founded on the unassailable principle that people learn best from doing.

Managerial Behavior

Aside from all that has been said about the absolute necessity of formal training in modern enterprise, it must be acknowledged that one of the most subtle educational influences in administration is the behavior of top management on the job. With all due regard for the independent-mindedness of the average employee, there is ample evidence that he takes his cues from his supervisory officials—more than from any other source. What managers do is infinitely more important in its effect on employees than what they say. This is no derogation of the intelligence or spirit of public workers; indeed, it is a testimonial to their perspicacity, to their immunity against being misled or fooled.

The style of management itself casts shadows over the organization that are scarcely paralleled by any other environmental factor. What one level of management does lower levels imitate. The brand of supervision, the mode of leadership, is far more influential than any doctrine espoused in a supervisory or human relations training course. Regard for ethics and the public interest is most persuasively taught by what top managers do, rather than by what they advocate.

In short, as has so often been said, management is training. To look upon training as something extraneous or superimposed is as much a mistake as looking upon any facet of the managerial process as having no educational impact. The character and magnitude of those activities that mold and develop employee performance lie not only in the techniques of formal training but in all aspects of management itself—and particularly in the attitudes and behavior of government's key managers.

And so the final caveat on this subject is to stress the necessity for training of managers themselves. The wise executive takes every opportunity available to learn more not only about his job and responsibilities but more about the environment in which his program operates and its relation to others, more about the organizing of human effort, and more about the leadership of human beings who have independent wills and aspirations of their own. Such a manager seeks every possible exposure that will enrich his experience and extend his perspective. He does this with full realization that his primary mission is leadership —a subject to which, in more specific terms, we now turn.

6

Leadership, Evaluation, and Discipline

BEFORE THE nineteen thirties such terms as "motivation" and "participation" were rarely heard in managerial circles in business or in government. "Scientific management," "efficiency," "economy"—yes, but few and far between were the expressions of concepts that today are commonplace in preparing executives to face the inexorable human problems of organization. Probably the most significant development in personnel administration in the mid-century period has been the widespread recognition of the critical importance of attention to human satisfactions in the work place, to individual differences, and to stimulating the will to achieve.

Earlier in this century bureaus of efficiency, particularly in our cities, concentrated on procedural and mechanistic approaches to productivity. The scientific management school of thought advocated finding and employing the "one best method" in every work process. Meanwhile, most managers—both public and private—

operated on the "Theory X" principle: that employees had to be driven or cajoled into productive effort. It was not until the landmark Hawthorne Works studies of the Western Electric Company at the end of the twenties that an approach based on studies of human behavior began to change the whole rationale and style of leadership in modern organization.

As a result, almost every aspect of personnel management—from day-to-day supervision to systems for reward and punishment—has been affected. In less than four decades the literature on this subject has assumed prodigious proportions. The image of the boss has evolved from one of a hard-driving, heartless Simon Legree to an understanding, insightful leader who is concerned about wedding the psychological needs of his employees with the goals of the enterprise.

Contrary to some assumptions, the net effect has not been to foster a namby-pamby, sweetness-and-light approach to direction of human effort but rather a hardheaded, realistic approach that understands the wellsprings of human motivation and consciously directs supervisory and employee behavior so as to capitalize on that understanding. What is this approach all about? On what fundamental concepts does it rest? How does it affect performance evaluation, discipline, and performance itself? What are the implications for managers at all levels? These are some of the questions to which this chapter is addressed.

What We Know About the "Climate"

No one should pretend that he can account for all the factors that influence human behavior or effort—even when attention is confined to conditions in the work place; for we have by no means mastered or fully comprehended all that is known about human psychology. We are dealing with the most complex thing on earth—man. But this need not dissuade us from going as far as we can in systematic study of man's behavior and of his reactions to various conditions of his environment. Equally formidable challenges faced us in landing a man on the moon, but we made that!

The fact is that much more is understood about human behavior than most of us are inclined to admit. Some of our reluctance to acknowledge and give effect to what we know—and to invest in further explorations —grows from the nature of the subject; it is one on which all of us have certain prejudices and fixed notions that we do not like to risk upsetting. Phenomena of the material world do not evoke stereotypes to the same extent; we are more willing to experiment with them, to revise ideas, and to try new methods. The striking thing about the new science of human behavior, as one student has observed, is: "not the vast areas of what is unknown—which many are fond of emphasizing—but the degree to which what is known is not used." This statement was made in 1949; and many advances and insights have been added since then. Whether putting these insights into practice has kept pace is debatable.

We cannot be as positive about the human factor as we can about the law of gravity, we cannot measure behavior as we can the speed of a rocket, but we can, with some confidence, isolate a few principles or concepts that have emerged from research and experience. Nor do we need to be absolutely complete in our articulation of these conclusions; if there are still areas of uncertainty and speculation, so be it. Let us, at least, make the most of how far we have come in understanding the behavior, motivation, and performance of man where he is involved in organized productive effort. And let us also remember that most of this knowledge can be applied by the ordinary manager of a government office, laboratory, hospital, or other facility.

Treating People as Adults

Among the more recent researches conducted in large organizations, there have been some that reveal a tendency by managers to treat adult subordinates as if they were children. This pattern of supervision is evidenced in several ways: assuming that employees need to be told precisely how to perform every task, without allowing any room for ingenuity; attributing low motivation to employees; discounting their judgment; indicating by little signs that they are not trusted to use good sense; over-review of their work; refusal to tolerate deviations from previous patterns of performance, even when they are proved at least as good as the old methods; failure to delegate authority that is called for by the manner in which clientele are being served; and so on.

The old adage of wise politicians vis-a-vis the voters is applicable to workers: "Never overestimate their knowledge, but never underestimate their intelligance." Equiping employees with the information they need to perform adequately is one thing; treating them as if they have little intelligence or will of their own is quite another. As we observed in the discussion on assignment of work, most people thrive on the sense of achievement they derive from productive effort. They are deprived of that satisfaction if they are denied latitude to make decisions on their own, to plan their own work, or to find little ways to do it better. This is why "management by objectives" is so important.

As far as work processes and technique will permit, it is always better to set goals and judge workers on the basis of results, rather than to over-prescribe methods and judge them by their degree of conformance. This was the fatal mistake of the early efficiency experts—devotees of that pseudo-scientific school of thought that proclaimed there was "one best way" of doing everything and that each worker should be required to use that way. This thesis overlooked the fact that there was one best way for *each worker,* and therefore a vast variety of best ways. This is why assembly lines in manufacturing industry have had to be substantially altered, why diversity and individual latitude have had to be introduced in every possible way.

The temptation of every manager who has been a successful individual performer is to view his supervisory job as being one of molding his subordinates into his own style. This doesn't work—at least not for long. The sooner he recognizes that each employee is a different individual, with his own God-given talents and quite capable of dealing with old tasks in new ways, the sooner he is able to treat subordinates as adults. And the sooner he will find— perhaps to his surprise—that there are ways of getting things done successfully that had never occurred to him.

Participative Management

Not quite the same but closely related is the matter of securing the participation of employees in achieving organization goals. The climate created by top management in this regard can make all the difference in the world in the spirit and productivity of an enterprise. Here we are thinking not merely of reliance on people to perform their individual jobs but of their broader contribution to the total organization.

Participative management exists when managers regularly and conscientiously seek out the ideas of their subordinates on solving policy problems, on making changes that should occur in work aims or processes, and on accommodating to changes in external circumstances or in clientele demands. It exists when the manager thinks of his own role as that of a coordinator of innovation, with his staff as the key innovators—not just himself. Not that he should not create or prod or challenge, but simply that he should exploit to the fullest the potential for creativity among his own colleagues.

A variety of devices are available to implement such an approach to management. For example, regular staff meetings, instead of being occasions for handing out instructions and orders, can be problem-solving sessions where each participant is encouraged to express his reactions and ideas. Task forces of employees can be appointed to explore specific issues and report back their conclusions or solutions. Draft proposals can be circulated for individual or group comment and recommendation. Suggestion systems can be directed toward meaningful aspects of the organization's functions and problems instead of toward such matters as ventilation, car parking, or coffee-breaks. The opportunities are almost endless for generating a feeling among the staff that their ideas are worthy of attention and that their participation in the difficult task of managing the enterprise is eagerly sought.

The important point to emphasize is that participative management depends almost entirely on the *attitude* of the manager, not just on technique. No amount of exploitation of devices and methods will produce much if employees detect that the manager's heart is not in it. Employees, being for the most part clever human beings, have an uncanny capacity for detecting such insincerity. On the other hand, the manager who is genuinely interested in his staff, who really respects their abilities and their judgment, and who earnestly wants their participation in his hard task of making the organization function effectively, will seldom fail to enlist the wholehearted support and the devoted respect of his staff.

The modern manager of governmental programs is not a lonely, beleaguered martyr, beset with insoluble problems, badgered by irresponsible subordinates; he is not an isolated figure in his private sanctum writhing over who is about to do what to him next—not, that is, if he is mindful of the power, the help, and the joy that is potentially available in that reservoir of capacity known as his staff. If he has faith in his fellow man, and recognizes that his staff consists of a representative sample, he will have no difficulty experiencing the enormous satisfactions that can come from leading an organization to effective performance.

Relation to Organization of Tasks

Only a word needs to be added to relate this discussion of managerial climate in an organization to the earlier discussion of organizing and assigning work. The most important single avenue for giving effect to the principles of supervision enunciated here is the manner in which responsibilities and daily tasks are divided, interrelated, and assigned. In fact, to add emphasis to what is being said about treating people as adults and about participative management, a rereading of the chapter on organizing and assigning work is strongly recommended. Note that the considerations that should be taken into account to permit employees to get the maximum motivation from their work and those that contribute to economical organization and performance are wholly consistent with the findings on leadership and managerial behavior in general.

Setting High Standards

A common mistake made in interpreting modern industrial psychology and behavioral research is to assume that their findings run counter to high expectations for productivity and quality performance. Perhaps there was a time, in the not too distant past, when some misguided enthusiasts mistook what was being learned as support for a kind of social-welfare approach to supervision. Because of such connotations that adhered to the phrase, the term "human relations" is avoided in this volume.

Researchers have also talked about "employee-centered supervision" and have stressed the need for concern with employee aspirations and feelings; and this was interpreted by some as a "be-kind-to-employees" mode of supervision. This was not intended by those who had conducted the research or who had first elucidated the conclusions; they were mainly bent upon discrediting old-fashioned notions that had failed to ascribe to employees any desire to work at all.

The researchers certainly did not produce evidence that one should not expect too much of employees; on the contrary. If behavioral research has demonstrated anything, it has shown that workers get satisfaction out of what they do only when they consider it worthwhile, when it challenges them, and when they can enjoy the exhilaration of exerting their capacities to the fullest. Far from condoning an easy-going, low-expectation level of operation, modern leadership psychology is grounded on the utility of high standards. If people acquire their greatest satisfactions in achievement, it follows that they will get more satisfaction from high quality than from mediocre achievement. There is not much kick in doing a poor job; but there is tremendous psychic compensation in doing a superior job. If someone has not already said that excellence (like virtue) is its own reward, then it ought to be said. Every thoughtful manager can testify to this truism from his own personal experience. His problem is in recognizing that it applies to his subordinates as well.

Thus, expecting—indeed demanding—the best from people is entirely practicable and consistent with the precepts emerging from modern behavioral research and modern management. To do less than setting high standards of performance is flying in the face of the wisdom we have gleaned from cumulative experience and patient, systematic inquiry. Managers, especially in government's critical responsibilities, have an obligation, not merely an opportunity, to set high standards and expect the best of their staffs.

It does not follow that the way to establish high standards and expectations is by fiat and arbitrary pronouncement. There is even such a thing as expecting too much. Completely unrealistic standards may, by setting goals that seem utterly unattainable, demoralize employees and have an inverse effect on productivity. The safest procedure, especially when there is no fixed tradition or objective method of establishing work standards, is to enlist the participation of the workers themselves in defining how much and what caliber of their product or service should be considered acceptable. Rarely, under such procedures, have employees come up with goals that were less than those envisaged by management alone; and frequently the goals have been higher. Chances are, also, that the goals will not be unrealistic.

Management will definitely find no excuse in the teachings of behavioral psychology for slipslod methods and mediocre work. Of course, there may be other explanations for low standards: poor selection of candidates, inadequate training, absence of incentives, union pressure, and the like. But any such deficiencies can be dealt with individually. Certainly any manager, employee, or union that tolerates mediocrity, pampers laggards along with producers, or fails to deal forthrightly with poor performance is contributing unwittingly to the erosion of our very civilization. But more about this later.

Permissiveness and Decisiveness

Another mistaken assumption about modern manage-

107

ment precepts is that decisiveness and aggressiveness are passé. There seem to be notions abroad that managers need not be strong, that inability to make up one's mind is no handicap, that the participative approach will take care of things, with employees carrying on while the supervisor serves as a kind of tolerant father figure who contributes little. Of course this is as spurious as the idea that low standards are all we can expect.

One of the saddest pretexts for a manager is one who is unable to make decisions. For no matter how much he relies on the participation and contribution of others, there will always be points—and usually very important ones—where he alone must make up his mind and render a judgment. The most common example is where there is division among his staff and colleagues over some issue and the solution is within his own jurisdiction. The weak official toys with the problem, speculates, and procrastinates—and generates little or no respect from any quarter. The strong manager makes certain that all who are entitled to it have had their say, assures himself that the facts are all in, ponders any ethical considerations that may be involved, and forthrightly makes a decision. Chances are he will make some people unhappy, but his capacity as an administrator and his integrity as a man will be unquestioned.

Perhaps this is the best place to underscore the point that good leadership does not consist simply of making people happy, or even contented; it consists of keeping them interested, putting them on their mettle, and challenging them. Permissiveness in giving employees all the rope they can handle, in enlisting their fullest powers and viewpoints, should not be confused with indecisiveness. An effective leader is not an automaton, without a mind of his own. He is more likely to be a fairly strong-willed person, confident in his own prowess and willing to put his judgments on the line; at the same time he is able to respect the interests, virtues, and wisdom of others and to make full use of these assets, especially in individuals from whom he expects collaboration in achieving common goals. In the long run perhaps, such behavior induces the greatest happiness for the greatest number.

Evaluating and Correcting Performance

Getting work accomplished is not simply a matter of setting goals and hoping for the best. There is always the hard task of deciding whether the goals have been met and what to do about it when they have not. One of the most intractable and yet inescapable aspects of personnel administration is the evaluation of performance, especially when it is applied to individuals. The reference here is not to forms and methods of evaluation but to the judgments themselves.

This is not the place for an extended discussion of alternative methods of performance evaluation; this will have to be left to more specialized publications. Of more immediate relevance to the concerns of operating managers is an analysis of some of the problems and pitfalls of evaluation, with suggestions as to what may be done to avoid them. Implicit in this discussion is also the issue of discipline.

What to Appraise

If a plan for employee appraisal focuses on personal traits and charactertistics, the chances are it is missing its target. The purpose should not be to assess the whole man but simply to gauge his performance. Sweeping (and usually ill-founded) judgments about a worker's personality or efforts to label his behavioral reactions for all time are beside the point; what's more, they are presumptuous and dangerous. Thus, attempts to rate broad traits—like initiative, cheerfulness, integrity, industriousness, or intelligence—might well be avoided.

The only legitimate concern of the supervisor is what the employee actually does. Therefore evaluation should always be directed at the facts of performance: the quality and quantity of work. Even where these are of an intangible nature, the factors considered should at least be in such terms. Where organization-wide rating systems are involved, managers should work to minimize trait appraisal and maximize job-performance appraisal.

It is well that managers eschew "playing God". It is difficult enough to appraise performance objectively and completely, without trying to assess things about a person that job performance does not fully or accurately reveal.

Over-Simplification

In an effort to simplify and regularize evaluations, personnel people have tended to put too many eggs in one basket. One evidence of this is their reliance on a single tool to serve multiple purposes. Evaluation systems that seek to provide a record for future promotion comparisons, for determining who should be retained on occasions of staff retrenchment, for making salary increases within a grade level, and perhaps for other purposes, are not likely to serve any one of those purposes well. Even at the expense of having to make more appraisals, managers are better off (and will be more satisfied with the results) if they go to the trouble of making special reports for each objective. When candidates are under consideration for promotion, the best time to make appraisals is on that particular occasion, so that they may report performance that is relevant to the job to which promotion is involved. This may, of course, take into account the total performance history of the individual. Similarly, if staff reductions are in process, evaluation should be in terms of gauging which employees can best be used on the remaining work.

Another rigidity that must be overcome—growing out of efforts to simplify—is the practice of making evaluations throughout the organization for the same fixed time periods. Managers understandably rebel against concentrating formal appraisal reports at the same time. More importantly, these periods do not fit all situations. One occasion when a report is definitely needed is when supervisors change—so that there will be a record of each supervisor's appraisal of each employee in the unit. Likewise, when an employee transfers, there should be a report of record on his performance in the job vacated. Of course, everyone also should be assessed at some reasonable interval following his first assignment to a position.

These are the main occasions when evaluations are called for. The most serious abridgment of these precepts comes through the insistence on periodic appraisals year after year for employees who have served on the same job for an extended period. The chances of anything new being reportable are minimal. If there are changes in the individual's performance, provision can be made for special reports; but there is little point in requiring repetition of identical appraisals time and time again on the misguided principle that everyone should be treated the same. Every case is different! Standardized reports on everybody at the same time do not really treat everyone the same.

There is also the practice of summing up appraisals in neat, overall conclusions. Inventors of rating systems have a compulsion to have their processes wind up by pigeonholing all employees into nice, identifiable categories—whether these be expressed in adjectives (excellent, very good, good, and so forth), or in numerical ranges, percentages, or other fixed entities. More likely than not, such categorization tends to produce spurious results. The elements in an employee's performance are not necessarily susceptible to being added up or averaged out, especially for the purpose of comparison with other employees. Under this approach, Joe Doaks who excels in his written work but is poor at personal contacts might fall into the same category as Tom Jones who is a great negotiator but cannot write an effective letter. Obviously, the specifics of performance are the important considerations, not how these may be added up. Comparisons among employees which depend wholly on common categories of performance are likely to be pretty shallow and meaningless exercises.

It may mean more work in judging employees on separate occasions of promotion, retention action, or salary eligibility determination; but wise managers will find appraisal systems that emphasize specific elements in performance—and do not depend on conclusion ratings—to be more useful and meaningful for operating purposes.

Impact of Evaluation

A neglected area of personnel management has been the study of the effect of evaluation on employees and their performance. Individuals differ in their need for praise and their tolerance of criticism. Supervisors find themselves almost instinctively taking this factor into account when they report the results of their judgments, especially to the employees themselves.

There are occasions when employees need a sledge-hammer approach in order to be jolted into a realization of their shortcomings and the possibilities for improvement; but there are other employees with whom a more subtle and less blunt approach is essential. Some require repeated assurance of the acceptability of their work, while others are sustained for months at a time by one small pat on the back. These differences in people can be taken into account most effectively in the day-to-day relationships between supervisor and subordinate. Attention to them should certainly not be saved up for the time of formal reporting of ratings—for this may be too traumatic an occasion for both parties. In any event, the supervisor must make an evaluation with an eye to its effect on the person whose work is being appraised.

Nothing is to be gained by failure to disclose the facts. If performance is wanting, it is better to communicate this fact to the employee promptly than to postpone the unpleasant task. The evaluator should direct his remarks as well as his reports to the objective facts of performance, not to the employee's personality or characteristics. As we noted before, he should not leave the impression that he is talking about the "whole man", but only about that part of him evidenced in the work. With rare exceptions, workers can accept such comments without being upset. Of course, if criticism comes after years of silence on the point at issue, an employee will understandably be upset.

In the long run, there is no substitute for continuous and forthright consultation with employees about their work, whether it is good or bad.

The Probationary Period

One of the biggest mistakes of government executives with substantial supervisory responsibility is to fail to make careful appraisals of performance during employee probationary periods. Many a later headache could have been avoided by prompt and full appraisal during the early months of an employee's assignment. There is not much more to say about this except to emphasize the common prevalence of this oversight and to underscore that for its consequences, which are many and sad, the offending managers have no one to blame but themselves.

113

The Fortitude to Fire

Related but not the same is the common reluctance to separate employees from duties to which they do not seem to be suited or on which they do not apply themselves with sufficient diligence or talent to meet reasonable standards. After full discussion with an individual performing unsatisfactorily—and after checking all possible remedies such as training, improving the motivational environment, elimination of personality clashes, and the like—if performance does not improve, it is the supervisor's obligation to do something about it. Sometimes correction can be made by transfer to other duties or to a new location, but unless these alternatives are really promising there should be no hesitation in presenting the individual with his walking papers.

A common complaint of managers is that it is too difficult to make such a firing "stick", that procedural requirements and appeals processes are too discouraging. Of course there are instances where the protections against incompetence and poor performance are too stringent and exasperating. If so, the official should stand up and fight for elimination of such unreasonable protections. Failing this, he should make sure that he has adequate records of specific events or work products to support his case when he must resort to a firing. Many a justifiable case is lost because the manager has not gone to the trouble of documenting the evidence.

However, for every instance where management is stymied by overindulgent laws and rules, there are at least two where the failure to fire is traceable simply to a lack of fortitude. Managing is a tough business; it is not for those who do not have the stomach for confrontations, nor the willingness to make unpleasant judgments and follow through with them. The first obligation of the public executive in this day when so much depends on the quality

of public services is to maintain high standards of performance. With all due consideration of the many factors involved in employee motivation and preparation for their
tasks—including a large role for the supervisor in creating
the climate for good performance—there will always be
cases where failure is clearly the responsibility of the employee. It is management's responsibility to see that he is
made accountable for that failure. Unfortunately, there
are unavoidable instances where there is no alternative to
dismissal.

Gauging Potential

Before leaving the subject of evaluation and its implications, mention must be made of one kind of appraisal that is not necessarily focused on performance.
Many public jurisdictions in recent years have asked their
managers to judge not only past achievement but how they
see each employee's future. This policy has been most
often applied to middle-level manpower with the intent of
maintaining a kind of perpetual inventory of talent for
higher managerial posts.

Some considerations that hedge about the assessment of
past performance do not apply here. In this case the organization is asking the manager to take into account the
past but also to make a highly subjective estimate of how
he thinks an employee is likely to develop, in other words
what he thinks of his "potential". This is, of course, risky
business; but who else is in a better position to make such
estimates than those who are paid to supervise and look
ahead?

Instead of foregoing the value of such judgments, however subjective and hazardous they might be, it behooves
management to find ways to offset possible errors or capri-
ciousness that might creep into the process. This can be
done, as mentioned in an earlier chapter, by spreading the

115

responsibility among several individuals. Thus, an appraisal of potential in any given case would be given no credence unless three or more supervisors of substantial rank had participated. In addition to those in the supervisory line, persons with lateral or service contacts with the subject employee could be called upon for judgments. It would be a pooling of these collective judgments that would be recorded rather than that of any one predictor alone. In this way, some perspective on the prospects among employees for future managers could be acquired without over-dependence on the labeling of an individual by one person.

Other Influences on Performance

Directing employee effort takes more than good leadership and careful evaluation, for a variety of other actions and conditions have their impact on performance. A few of the most important ones are taken note of here.

Pay Flexibility and Formal Incentives

To carry out management's total job requires more flexibility in pay scales than most public personnel systems provide. Initially, pay ranges for each individual grade level were designed to provide just such flexibility. Salary increases were to be earned. The better the performance, the more generous the increase; when performance was not sufficiently good to warrant such advancement, increases were to be denied.

Over the years, however, a great deal of automatism has crept into public pay policy—largely due to the political influence of government employee unions. Time and again unions have mistaken their mission on behalf of the worker to mean that they should reduce to the minimum any recognition of individual differences. To exorcise the bogey that supervisors might play favorites or use poor judgment, unions have persuaded too many legislatures and municipal councils that pay increases on a regular basis should go to all who are good enough to be kept on the rolls. The result in too many systems is that movement up the steps in a pay range becomes automatic with time-serving, passable performance being rewarded the same as superior performance—a condition that hardly provides an incentive for superior performance.

Nevertheless, many systems still permit some latitude for recognition of differences in performance. The problem in these instances is getting managers to use the flexibility they have. The positive feature in such flexibility is that more rapid or larger pay jumps may be given to outstanding employees. Usually such a procedure calls for some kind of special justification, but this is ordinarily not onerous. Or, a negative provision may be included, one that denies periodic advancement when work does not measure up to certain standards. There is considerable evidence that such flexibility pays off. Pay is by no means the only important incentive in a work situation, but it will always be one of the most important. To fail to use it for its incentive value does not bode well for the tone and quality of any organization.

Apart from pay scales, special money incentives are also available in many jurisdictions in the form of cash awards or bonuses given to individuals or groups of employees who excel in general performance or who have rendered some unusual service. The adoption of such award plans has somewhat offset the lack of flexibility in formal pay scales; however, a few jurisdictions have both. Some cynics are inclined to discount the utility of cash awards, but those organizations that have used them extensively can testify to their practical value.

Other forms of award and recognition can be just as

effective. Honors in the form of certificates, plaques, or medals—especially when publicly presented—can have a tremendous impact not only on the receiver but on those who witness the ceremony. There are few workers who do not get some thrill out of the public recognition that comes with an honor award.

There are doubters who maintain that awards do not inspire others to extraordinary effort because there are always disappointed employees who think they should have received the honor in preference to those recognized. But even when this is true only a tiny minority is likely to feel disgruntled (or have the audacity and conceit to consider themselves in the competition). And even if the feeling is widespread, it does not take away from the desirability of giving due recognition to superior achievement whether it inspires others to greater exertion or not. In other words, a policy of generous recognition of excellence is justifiable on its own merits, regardless of its incentive for others. Superiority should not be ignored just because there may be some rivals who will resent the recognition.

Scheduling Leave

One of the sensitive tasks of every supervisor is balancing the needs of the organization with the desires of employees in the timing of their vacations or other leaves. In small work units the problem almost solves itself; also, professional employees often check with each other and enter into a considerable amount of mutual coordination before confronting the supervisor with a need for reconciling requests. However, in large units where substantial numbers of employees are engaged in comparable duties and only a limited portion can be absent at any one time if the workload is to be handled properly, some formal scheduling of leave is necessary.

This is one of those areas of managerial decision-making which is admirably suited to employee participation. It concerns their own welfare, but employees cannot duck the organization's need to have a minimal workforce on hand at all times. This need is likely to induce a real sense of responsibility on the part of employees asked to work out the solution; and their participation is also likely to make the results more acceptable.

A variety of schemes for participation are available: a committee of workers, perhaps elected by them, might develop the leave schedule; or a series of alternative plans could be put to the entire group for vote; or blocks of vacation time might be parceled out to sub-units for each to distribute among its workers by its own democratic methods. In any event, the parameters and constraints in time and numbers would have to be set by management at the outset; the rest could be done by the employees themselves at least as well as by any manager.

Looking After Health

Industrial medicine has come into its own. The day has long passed when the health and safety of workers was considered an individual's personal responsibility, with the employer having no responsibility at all. Now every up-to-date enterprise has a positive program of health maintenance and injury treatment, to say nothing of a safety program. Having doctors and nurses on the permanent staff is commonplace in all large organizations.

The individual manager's role is clear. While he may not be directly responsible for providing professional medical or safety services, he must be ever conscious of their availability and utility; and he must be sensitive to situations where employees need health counseling. As for safety, part of it depends on engineering, but the greater

119

part depends on safe attitudes and an awareness of safety hazards. In these respects the manager sets the pattern for the alertness of those working with him.

Communication

A concluding word is appropriate on the subject of communication—the up-and-down dissemination of information and ideas, the lateral contacts with other parts of the organization, the informal as well as the deliberately designed interchange of facts, thoughts, opinions, and instructions. Much of what we have in mind is implicit in earlier discussions of leadership, participation, training, and work assignment. Communication is the life blood that makes the structure of organization function.

Every manager should think of his job as that of chief coordinator of communication. Reluctance to spend time at this job, reluctance to have employees spend time at meetings or otherwise learn what is going on, is very short-sighted. Workers who know about the rest of the organization are more likely to care about it; and caring is half of the job. Employees who feel they know what top management is thinking, who feel they have an open and ready communication channel with that management, are more likely to be alert and responsive. It is hardly necessary to repeat here the ways already enumerated in which good communication can be facilitated.

But one device has not yet been mentioned—the attitude survey. There is nothing new about it, and it is seldom written about except in technical journals; but it is one of the most useful techniques known to the personnel profession. It is the best and surest way to find out what employees are really thinking about—on any subject which is the proper business of the organization.

Management often thinks it knows what its workers think—and it is as often wrong. Supervisory managers are free to conduct surveys or have outsiders conduct them within their units at any time. They need not await the leadership of a personnel office. The subject of the surveys may be any of a number of things:

- viewpoints of employees on certain personnel practices;
- their feelings about the supervision and leadership they are getting (this is frequently an eye-opener!);
- their knowledge of the work aims of the enterprise;
- their acquaintance with related activities in other organizations;
- their interests in and interpretation of the desires and problems of the clientele groups served by the organization;
- their knowledge and concern for technological or sociological changes that affect their work;
- and so on.

Instead of relying on haphazard and spasmodic wisps of information that may drift up to the attention of top management, executives can facilitate the process of communication on a more systematic basis by occasional or even periodic analyses of what employees under their direction know and think. Attitude surveys require considerable professional care in the design of questionnaires and the planning of sample interviewing (where interviewing will add to understanding); and the analysis of results also calls for the sure touch of those who have been through the experience before. But the determination of what issues are most in need of survey is the responsibility of operating management. Sears, Roebuck, and Company is an example of a firm that employs attitude surveys on a regular basis to determine what is going on in the minds and hearts of its agents (from warehouse to retail store) as a basis for an annual reassessment of company policy. These are not primarily surveys of personnel policy attitudes but are explorations of problems that are part of the ebb and flow of daily operations.

Government agencies would do well to follow Sears' example. Attitude surveys have been used in isolated instances many times but almost never on a periodic basis; and probably the majority of public agencies have never had a survey at all. This is an omission that deprives operating executives of one of the vital tools of their trade—complete and accurate information from all levels in the organization. Reliance on natural capillary action is not enough.

Having made a survey, the action does not stop there; surveys are meaningless, even dangerous, if their results are given no attention and do not influence policy. Better that they not be conducted at all if management is not prepared to act upon them.

But managers should not fear such surveys. Even though results are sometimes surprising and some criticism of management almost inevitable, managers will find attitude surveys more than worthwhile because of the true measure they will most likely provide, if carefully conducted, of the pulse and tempo of the enterprise. Certainly it is safer for management to act on the basis of facts rather than on conjecture.

7

Employees in
the Corporate Sense

N OT ALL government executives are in a position to
negotiate with employee unions on major policy issues.
However, most executives are concerned with union behavior and frequently encounter union inquiries, requests,
complaints, or demands. In so doing they are dealing with
their employees not as individuals but as a body. Their
contacts are not necessarily with those who may work directly for them but rather with the latters' representatives.

Unionism in the Public Service

The fastest growing unions in the United States are
those in the public service—federal, state, and municipal.
Paralleling the growth of the public service itself, the
surge of government employee corporate consciousness
and accompanying unionism in the 1960s and 1970s may
be as significant as the expansion of labor organization in
private industry following the passage of the National
Labor Relations Act in the 1930s.

Unions, even in government employment, are of course much older than the 1930s. Organization of public workers followed mainly on the heels of unionization in the private sector, but some of today's government unions can claim an age approaching a century in length. Beginning in the latter quarter of the nineteenth century, municipal police and firemen, public school teachers, and federal postal workers have the distinction of being the first public employees to have organized to promote and protect their own welfare.

These groups are still among the most influential unions in the public sector, but growth is taking place more dramatically in the general-purpose, non-craft unions —like the American Federation of State, County, and Municipal Employees (AFSCME) and, in the federal service, the American Federation of Government Employees (AFGE), both affiliated with the American Federation of Labor—Congress of Industrial Organizations (AFL-CIO). Like their counterparts in industry, government workers have concluded that it is necessary or at least profitable to make their influence on public policy makers felt as a body. Whether they represent the interests of specific occupational segments of public employment or more generous cross-sections, government unions are a real-life phenomenon that government executives cannot ignore. Indeed, it behooves the manager in government service to understand the raison d'être and psychology of union organization and leadership and to find ways of working constructively with it—within the boundaries of his public responsibilities and his accountability to the commonweal.

Union Achievements and Roles

For one thing, the manager will have to note the fact that many constructive features of modern personnel policy are traceable to the initiative and support of employee organizations. In fact, some of the benefits that he personally enjoys as a public employee he may owe to the political power exerted by the union with which he must now negotiate. Traditionally government unions have supported the merit system, at least with reference to initial entrance to the service. In many localities and in the federal service unions were instrumental in getting adoption of position classification and retirement plans. And, to be sure, they have been a potent force in most places in bringing government salaries up to a level of decent comparability with those in private enterprise.

But the basis for unionism lies deeper. Even when good working conditions and pay have been solidly established, organization of employees proceeds apace. Other motives seem to require their banding together and to stimulate the flexing of their corporate muscles.

The larger and more impersonal bureaucracies become, the more their members (like those in large private corporations) sense a need for something that belongs to them alone. This the union often supplies. Employees need the satisfaction of doing something for themselves. Personnel policies handed out to them, even on the proverbial silver platter, are not quite the same as those which they had a part in shaping. Also, as a counterweight to the sameness of routine daily tasks, a voluntary employee organization offers an opportunity for satisfying social and leadership aspirations that the work in the office or shop may not make possible.

Finally, there is the significance of organization for purposes of communication. Many aspects of the employment relationship (pay, for example) are beyond the scope of authority of individual managers or even of executive agencies, considering the large role which legislative bodies have in personnel policy-making. A union makes it possible to synthesize employee viewpoints on these over-all matters and to express that consensus forcefully to the ultimate

125

decision-makers. Collective employee representation makes sense as a channel of communication for countless small voices which otherwise would likely never be heard. Even when last year's goals have been achieved, it remains a channel that requires continuous use in order to reassure employees that it is still there.

At the same time, this simplification and synthesis of communication with the rank and file provide a convenience to management. Because the union is initiated by and belongs to the employees, it can usually be depended upon to speak more certainly for them than is the case with the slow, and often faulty, distillation of opinion that may seep up the supervisory line. When government managers really want to know what employees as a body think about working conditions, the union provides a means for getting at the facts—at least as employees see them.

Some Shortcomings

Despite all these worthwhile purposes, it should not be surprising that unions have some deficiencies. Public employee union leadership has not always been of a high caliber or of sufficient maturity to bear real responsibility. Furthermore, this leadership has tended to overemphasize four employment practices that are hardly consonant with high quality performance:

- uniform treatment for all workers regardless of obvious differences in effort, initiative, or productivity.
- minimum instead of maximum or optimum accomplishment as the acceptable work standard.
- over-solicitude for and protection of poor performance.
- seniority as the major criterion for advancement.

In too many jurisdictions pressure for such policies has not convinced the general public that what travels under the banner of employee welfare is always for the public welfare.

There is considerable question whether employees are content with practices that run counter to natural motivation and inhibit maximum achievement. Unfortunately, as a long-lasting backlash against the malpractices and nepotism that were rampant in private business many decades ago, union leadership is still preoccupied with the notion that distinctions among workers must be erased. To do so, of course, not only flies in the face of that which makes an achieving society what it is but bodes ill for its future. One of the most constructive tasks that government executives could undertake would be to demonstrate to and convince union leaders that such practices as seniority, coddling of poor performers, and failure to recognize superior achievement are no more in the interest of long-run worker satisfaction than of organizational productivity.

Special Problems

In addition, unionism in the public service poses some problems not typical of unionism in private industry. Most of these grow out of unalterable conditions that should be faced realistically instead of being brushed aside.

Authority. Several aspects of the governmental power situation make it markedly different from that in the business arena. First of all, management in government is supposed to represent the public at large, not just a private owner or group of owners. Government, as such, is in an unassailably superior position to any body of its employees in a way that no private management can claim. The latter is just one of two equal parties before the law, while government is the originator, custodian, and implementer of the law. Government and its employees are not equal bargainers.

Second, most of the conditions of employment in government, especially pay, are prescribed by law. The executive arm of government is seldom free to set all the terms of employment in the sense that business management may. Third, there is a problem of ascertaining just where or who the "government" really is. Decision-making authority is much more diffused than in the private world; and purposely so—to avoid over-concentration of power. Neither does this fact of life make the position of the parties quite the same as in industry.

Membership. The original issues as to whether government employees could belong to unions at all and, if they could, whether such unions could be affiliated with the general labor movement have been answered in almost all jurisdictions with a resounding affirmative. But attempts at closer parallels with industrial practice in the matter of union membership are not so easy.

The "closed shop" (under which the union supplies all job candidates; prevalent only in limited kinds of industries) clearly contravenes the government's authority to hire, to say nothing of doing violence to the merit system. It is therefore unknown in the public service. The "union shop" (under which all employees hired must eventually join the union; more common in industry) has been accepted in a few American municipalities but so far has not made much headway. Another device (contrived especially for government) known as the "agency shop" (under which all employees hired must submit to a "check-off" of union dues from their pay checks whether they join the relevant union or not) has also won only limited acceptance.

Although the closed and union shops are cornerstones of industrial-union philosophy—inspite of their relatively narrow application—they betray a fundamental weakness in employee organization. The argument on their behalf is that employees who benefit from union representation should be forced to support the cause. But this position ignores the discipline of having an economic organization *earn* its strength. If a union cannot win the overwhelming support of the employees it purports to represent, of what

128

value is it as a representative agent? Also, a guarantee of membership is scarcely motivation for alert and aggressive union leadership.

Government executives should beware of union efforts to achieve even the agency shop, to say nothing of the closed shop or union shop. The closed shop is utterly incompatible with the merit idea and government hiring authority; and the other two forms of guaranteed membership are incompatible with voluntary representation of employee interests.

Representation. Unlike most private businesses, many governmental jurisdictions are beset with a multiplicity of unions seeking to represent the same groups of employees. Sometimes these are occupational craft unions, sometimes their coverage is general. Conflicts are common between the two forms of organization.

The manager of the public business who is faced with competing demands and competing employee leadership has only one recourse; he can refuse to accept any of the competitors until the employees themselves decide who shall represent them. Standard methods of conducting employee elections are widely available. Until a majority of employees in any particular unit, occupational or organizational, is prepared to name a specific union as its protagonist, management is under no obligation to deal with a union as the genuine agent of its workers. Of course, this is not to say that management has no obligation to seek out employee viewpoints and to take them into account in the formulation of administrative policy. Such responsibilities persist regardless of the degree of employee organization.

Strikes and Settlement of Disputes. The most disturbing and perplexing issue concerning government unionism is the use of the strike weapon. Traditionally government unions had foresworn the right to strike; and many jurisdictions forbade them outright. Nevertheless, strikes have occurred—and in recent years with increasing frequency, severity, and effect. So far, however, really serious dislocations resulting from strikes have been confined to comparatively few places.

The origin of the strike dates back to the industrial revolution, having developed as a necessary counter measure to oppressive behavior by employers who tended to think of workers as machines or animals. Eventually strikes became part of the arsenal of union actions designed to assure fair wages and decent working conditions. Until recent years the adverse impact of a strike was principally on a single employer and his workers; the consumer was able to turn to other alternatives for goods or services.

The theory underlying proscription of strikes in government was that most of its services were not supplied by alternative means and were so compelling or essential to the public interest that interruption was intolerable. The strikes that have occurred in police forces, public transportation, and schools certainly illustrate the dire consequences of work stoppages in such areas.

It can be argued, of course, that equally serious effects are visited upon the consuming public by strikes in many privately-operated services—airlines, railroads, bus lines, electric power, telephone communication, and the like. This argument could be used to support banning strikes in privately-owned public utilities with as much reason as it is used to support lifting the prohibition in government services. The real common denominator is this: under either circumstance a special responsibility rests on both government and public utility managers to maintain conditions of employment that will keep serious unrest from developing among the workers.

However, as has been said before, full power to control personnel policy is seldom in the hands of executives in government. Legislative bodies—ultimately the voters and taxpayers—usually set the basic conditions of pay, hours of work, fringe benefits, and other rewards and conditions of government employment. It is sad but true that the dissatisfaction of many civil servants over the years has been due to the niggardliness and negative attitudes toward them displayed by the American public. Under such circumstances in some jurisdictions it is understandable why some union leaders contend seriously for the right of public employees to strike.

Government managers have opportunities, too infrequently exploited, to contribute to the correction of poor working conditions and inadequate compensation. Instead of standing mutely by, in fear of their jobs, they should be among those fighting for improvement when the cause is just. Although they are at a psychological disadvantage, since they stand to gain personally from pay and other improvements, this embarrassment is not compelling enough to offset their obligation to demonstrate to legislators and the general public how and to what degree the working environment and employee compensation warrant change. Unless they do so they leave the battle only to the unions.

Furthermore, when things do come to an impasse, managers can contribute to attitudes of toleration and willingness to negotiate. Their recognition of genuine employee concerns and their receptivity to open and honest discussion can create an atmosphere conducive to settlement instead of contributing to the extreme resort of a work stoppage. They have the opportunity of formulating and suggesting machinery for adjudication or arbitration—recognizing that the latter must be set up within the framework of government itself. In spite of the recalcitrance of legislative bodies and the reluctance of taxpayers leagues, executives in government as a class can do much to alleviate conditions that might trigger a strike.

Nevertheless, there will always be situations where strikes are fomented for reasons that government managers cannot condone. The only real deterrents to such service interruptions are: effective constraints on union leadership and union treasuries, and insistence on enforceable third-party arbitration (within the machinery of government) to settle unresolved issues. When well-paid employees are misled into thinking that they are justified in demanding still more pay, when union leadership engineers work stoppages in jurisdictional disputes, when unions seek to control the substantive policies and operations of a government agency, some curb on strikes seems unavoidable. In the last analysis the general public is the boss. The public interest cannot be placed in jeopardy by the minority that it has employed to carry on its collective services. Unless every conceivable means are used to avoid those conditions that give rise to employee unrest, unless every restraint is exercised to prevent work interruptions, the current rash of strikes in government—justified or not —will be an overture to chaos.

Working With Unions

The average government manager is not faced every day with these special problems of unionism; rather, he is more likely to encounter formal employee representation in a more mundane way: in frequent opportunities for communication, painstaking give and take, and efforts at agreement.

Utility of Representation

We have already observed that the fact of employee representation through unions can be advantageous to management. When service-wide personnel policies are under discussion, the union provides a convenient means for insuring that the employee viewpoint will be heard. Not only may the responsible executives benefit from the ideas of employee groups and their representatives, but incorporation of many of their proposals may avoid pitfalls that would not have been perceived by management alone. The very process of consultation and involvement of employee representatives in the planning stages of personnel policy development paves the way for better understanding and acceptance of change where change is needed. Moreover, the habit of consultation promotes a continuing relationship of mutual understanding and reduces the potential for conflict.

Communication

In the preceding chapter attention was given to some aspects of communication within a complex enterprise. Another facet of this subject is evidenced in regular consultation and negotiation between management and unions.

The primary and overriding lesson to be learned from this relationship is the necessity for a policy and practice of openness. Clandestine planning of personnel policy changes by management alone rarely results in sound planning. Chances are that it will only evoke suspicion, charges of secretiveness and ulterior motives, and resistance to making the results effective. The day when the executive group could determine conditions of employment of their subordinates without the latters' participation has long ago passed. It is a cardinal tenet of any democratic environment that those affected by decisions must have some say in their making. Disclosure of management objectives and free discussion with all affected parties constitute the only ways in which relevant considerations can be taken into account and the ultimate success of a prospective policy insured.

In addition to managerial initiatives that must be shared with unions, proposals by the employee organizations themselves must be given serious and genuine consideration. However farfetched or impracticable they may at times seem (sometimes due to inexperience), they establish a basis for negotiation. Brushing them aside accomplishes nothing. If they are in fact impossible of achievement, management's most effective posture is to demonstrate this clearly and then to offer more practical alternatives.

Most government executives are conditioned to a regular flow of inquiries from the press and the general public; they are accustomed to operating within a goldfish bowl. They are not dismayed by criticism or startled by resistance from outside the organization. What some of them have not yet learned to accept is the same concern, inquisitiveness, and suspiciousness, the same desire to express a point of view, on the part of those within the organization.

It does not speak well for managerial sensitivity to employee interests when the agency's workers first learn of some intention or action by management through the public press. Quite apart from matters of personnel policy, any new element or circumstance that will affect daily operations had best be divulged within the organization before it is pronounced to the world. Employees who are expected to implement it are entitled to be first in the know. Even when decisions or facts are not the kind requiring consultation with employee groups, common sense suggests the desirability of clarification within the family first. Otherwise there can be no sense of common purpose or mission, no feeling that there *is* a "family".

Negotiation—A Way of Life

Getting the Union View. The modern government manager accepts consultation and, where appropriate, negotiation with unions as a way of life. His first question to staff members revising personnel policies or methods is:

"What are the plans for checking this out with the unions?" He follows through with insistence on a full exploration of union views, and finally on careful weighing whether reasons for any disagreement with the employee organizations are valid and defensible.

In instances where one union represents a clear majority of employees in a given work unit, the potentiality of written agreement between management and union must be considered. Such agreements may cover any personnel policy subject within the province of executive management—such as pay adjustments within grade levels, scheduling of leave, bases and procedures for promotion, safety measures, hearing of employee grievances, and processing disciplinary actions.

The negotiating process is dependent more on an attitude and an approach than on the application of basic rules. Many jurisdictions have laws establishing the framework for collective representation of employees, for negotiation and bargaining, and for written agreements. However, the real success of the relationship lies in willingness by both parties to listen to the other side, give real consideration to the facts and viewpoints presented, and modify original positions where circumstances warrant. Mutual trust and real effort at understanding the other fellow's stance can go far to lubricate the way to a common settlement.

Role of Personnel Office. When subjects of organization-wide import are involved, the logical unit to handle the details of negotiation is the personnel office. If there is any question about its competence to take the leadership in sensitive negotiations, then its ability to handle any part of the personnel program is in question. The personnel office that is expected to process papers only and is not considered able to speak for management is not worthy of the name. The subject of negotiations and agreements is the

135

very essence of personnel administration; and those who spend full time on that subject matter should have the primary competence in it.

Role of Managers. Nevertheless, operating managers cannot be absolved of responsibility in this area. Where they are at the apex of the organization for which negotiations are being conducted, they must back the personnel officials, not only in resisting impossible demands but in accommodating to well-supported contentions. On the most critical issues they may have to participate directly in discussions with union representatives—but not in a manner or with a continuity that undermines the authority or effectiveness of those designated to represent management regularly.

Managers who deal frequently with union representatives must be well-informed about the patterns and pitfalls of negotiation. They must acquaint themselves with union traditions and attitudes. They must, above all, be fully cognizant of their own prerogatives and their responsibility at all times to interpret and defend the public interest. Special training programs designed to facilitate such managerial understanding are available from several sources and could well serve as part of the formal preparation of all supervisory personnel who take part in negotiation sessions with unions.

Obligation toward Merit. Moreover, government executives will have to stand fast, along with the personnel professionals, in protecting the merit system. Some misguided union leaders have sought to substitute collective bargaining agreements for the laws by which a jurisdiction governs entry into its service. Merit procedures should always be open to improvement, but the principle of merit as the basic criterion should never be compromised, nor should the means necessary to attain true merit. Hiring under union agreements simply substitutes union patronage for political party patronage. It is as much the business of operating officials to protect the merit principle (and the wherewithal to maintain it) as it is of the personnel office.

Managerial Behavior. Finally, the responsibility of general government managers is reflected in their everyday behavior and actions. Much of what unions are concerned with grows out of the quality of supervision and direction given to the work force. Many of their complaints, or efforts to forestall actions inimical to employee interests, develop out of experience with the operating line. Thus, what goes on in day-to-day relationships between supervisors and workers has, as we already emphasized, a major impact on employee attitudes and on what they communicate to their representatives. Keeping his own house in order personnel-wise is not only necessary to insure the manager's compliance with pertinent rules and controls, it is good business in forestalling difficulties with employee unions.

The Public's Obligation

This chapter should not be closed without reiteration of the general public's responsibility to underwrite and support sound personnel administration in its public services. The desperation and militancy of some government unions can be traced directly to neglect by the American public of its public servants. The "open-season" attitude towards bureaucrats, the unwillingness in so many jurisdictions to pay the price for a quality staff, the thoughtless and wholesale criticism that is so often directed against government employees, combine to explain a "fed-up" response and determination by those so abused to wrest recognition from their detractors.

There is no alternative to fair pay and decent working conditions in our public services. Unless these are maintained on a par with those prevailing in at least the average or better private industries, continued trouble with government employee organizations can be taken for granted. The citizen who thinks of government only as some leech on the body politic and of taxes as waste down the drain, yet demands ever-increasing services from government, inhibits the efficiency that he claims to favor. No amount of hand-wringing over "militant labor" in government will change its impact. Far more effective would be a searching examination to see if the employment situation could be improved. When the public conscience is clear, then and only then is the public entitled to question the tactics of government unions.

In bringing the man on the street to a realization of his responsibilities, the government manager can contribute much. He can seize every opportunity to display the good works of his staff, to call attention to deficiencies in their treatment by the taxpayer, and to testify before legislative committees concerning his agency's personnel program needs. When he is an expert in a field of work in which the average citizen patently has a stake, his word can be influential. He should not shrink from articulating the case for the civil servant. He needs only to be convinced of the justice of his cause.

8

Some Public Policies
to Live With

NO AMOUNT of rhetoric will convince the sophisticated government manager that every feature of the
personnel system in his jurisdiction is designed to contribute to the effectiveness of his management. And, chances
are, he will be right. For many requirements and constraints are matters of public purpose and are not particularly motivated by the goal of efficiency. This fact does
not, however, reduce the manager's responsibility for complying with these limitations.

In fact, it adds another kind of obligation: whenever
he can demonstrate that such restrictions interfere with
the successful or economical rendering of the services with
which he is charged, he should be in the forefront of the
fight to get them changed. Complaining to those who have
little power to effect corrections gains little. The executive
responsible for a government program must be prepared
to champion unpopular causes against popular adversaries.
Taking such risks is the essence of responsibility; shrink-

139

ing from them means that he is a spineless minion, the
epitome of the classical concept of the "government clerk."

Political Direction and Control

The most fundamental parameter within which government executives operate is that of political leadership.
Even when the program manager himself is a political
appointee, he sometimes chafes at the demands and concerns of party leadership.

The Democratic System

There are some basic "givens" in democracy that are
inescapable. Elected officials must have the power and
means to control the administrative machinery of government; otherwise there is no point to their election. However weak or strong, misguided or inspired, evil or good
they may be, they are the bosses when they are in power.
The electorate deserves what it puts into office. And it
must learn from its mistakes.

Fortunately, most elected officials mean to do the right
thing—to serve the broad public interest as they see and
interpret it. They may misgauge the situation and make
mistakes; but, by and large, the burdens of public office
have a way of bringing out the best in people. For the most
part public officials try their best to solve the problems that
beset modern man. As some cynics would have it, they are
often held in an upright position by conflicting pressures
from opposing sides.

There is a difference, however, between the role of the
legislator and that of the elected or appointed political
executive. The leader in the executive role is in a far more
responsible and exposed position than the average legislator. The latter is protected by numbers and is not pinned

down to a specific program; he is free to shift his emphasis and his interests. Whatever he does, he is only one among many. When his cause fails, he can say he had only one vote; when it succeeds, he can claim credit for it without much challenge from others. The political executive, on the other hand, is top dog in his particular bailiwick. Decisions cannot so readily be ducked. What's more, he is directly responsible for the actions and behavior of all those who work within his organizational unit. The public tends to think of him as all-powerful—however little real leverage he may have.

Career Responsibility

The point of all this is that political executives deserve all the support, benefit of the doubt, and loyal performance from career civil servants that the latter can muster. Whenever career employees conclude that they are justified, as a matter of right and as they deem necessary, in taking matters into their own hands and defying their political leaders, they are weakening the sinews of democracy. Any assumption that they rather than the voters have the right to determine ultimate policy is a denial of government by the people. If loyal responsiveness to political leadership is unconscionable to career employees, they have the option of leaving their posts and entering the arena of public advocacy known as "politics." Only when the orders or actions of their leaders are so patently illegal or unethical that there would be no doubt of it among reasonable men are they in a proper position to defy that leadership and stay on the job.

The Legislative Role

Political leadership on the legislative side is of a different ilk. In most countries legislatures spend their full

141

time on matters of policy and law; they seldom if ever tamper with the methodology of getting things done. In fact, in some nations the bulk of personnel policy is an executive matter, governed only in very general terms by law. The tradition in the United States— a tradition which has hampered the development of modern administrative methods and at times jeopardized managerial responsibility—has been for the legislative bodies to occupy themselves with all kinds of management detail, to overprescribe precisely how transactions should take place, to restrict and hamstring administrators in all kinds of ways, under the simple-minded notion that the best way to insure a certain brand of implementation of a public policy is to "write it in the law."

Actually the best and most effectively administered policies in our history have been those in which wide latitude was left to the executive side of government—not those where every "t" of application was crossed and every "i" of anticipated effect was dotted. The complexity of modern government does not permit wise anticipation of all the administrative problems that are going to be encountered when a new program or policy is established. There must be room for accommodation to the unexpected, for adaptation to change in circumstances and environment. Too many of our laws do not provide such room.

Nevertheless, when a law is on the books, it is public policy that must be heeded. It is not for administrators to decide whether they will obey the law. To follow it in spirit and in letter is their sworn duty—whether they consider it sound or not.

At the same time, administrators are bound to make known to legislators what they find wrong with the law, both substantively and in its administrative features. For the most part, legislators will listen to reason. They will especially pay attention to persuasive explanations as to why a program should be administered differently. How else are they going to get the executive viewpoint unless executives express it? The chief problem is in getting government managers to screw up the courage to present their case and to present it effectively. In their anxiety to maintain good relations with the legislature, they often refrain from constructive criticism, only to have their reluctance backfire later on when someone else calls attention to the deficiency. The legislator's natural query then is: "Why didn't you tell us before?"

Needless to say, personnel laws are often among those statutes that could stand improvement in their administrative provisions. Both operators and personnel people share the responsibility for showing how it can be done.

The Courts

The third branch of the American governmental structure is the judiciary. Its degree of involvement in personnel matters varies from jurisdiction to jurisdiction but in a number of places it is heavily involved indeed.

The courts get into the personnel business when individuals or groups challenge the legality or constitutionality of some administrative action. Thus, disappointed candidates for employment sometimes question the appropriateness of a test; dismissed employees contest their separation; unions sue for recognition; job seekers challenge certain bars to their entry to examination; or any of a variety of other suits are filed to bring about some change in a practice which a plaintiff finds inimical to his personal interest. The contested practice may or may not be inappropriate or unfair, and it may or may not have any proper legal foundation. The question usually decided by the courts is whether the action or rule is within the authority of the responsible administrative agency or whether it is arbitrary or capricious.

143

In the great majority of cases adjudication has cleared the air of any doubt about a government agency's power and reasonableness in handling personnel matters. In a few cases it has properly called public administrators to task for exceeding or misusing their authority. In still other cases, however, there has been a tendency for judges to interpret laws extremely narrowly or without insight into the world of administration. The result has been the encasement of many personnel systems in intricate webs of legalisms that serve no good purpose. Such instances only encourage future litigation and keep lawyers busy contending over fine points of procedure, completely missing the substance of wholesome administration.

Some members of the judiciary seem to view all relationships, including those between manager and employee, in the context of adversary proceedings. Most of them, however, dismiss efforts to reduce management to this status by recognizing the latitude that government managers must have if they are to respond to the *intent* of the laws they administer and if they are to do so with reasonable efficiency.

In any event, the decisions of the courts are real-life constraints to which administrators must pay heed; they have the force and effect of law. When the decisions seem utterly unreasonable or unworkable, the only recourse is a change in legislation or even in a constitution. In such instances, once again, we encounter the necessity for public executives to be prepared to support, even initiate, the changes.

The Power of the Bureaucracy

From what has been said one might mistakenly infer that the average government manager is an overly-restricted, abused creature—beset on all sides by demanding political leaders, unsympathetic legislators, and pettyfogging judges. If this were the typical situation, certainly very little effective public administration would ever be accomplished. But the fact is that much good work does emanate from the bureaucracy; and administrators do exercise great power.

The public executive who cries loudest over his plight is not always the one who is really suffering; sometimes he simply does not wish to accept his responsibility for operating within the policy and legal frameworks prescribed by a democracy. To be sure, he is not free to give vent to his personal will; and he must not ignore the rights of individuals, within or outside his agency. He must achieve stated program ends by certain specified means. However, he may fail to appreciate the enormous influence he has—even within these basic requirements. He may not sense the overwhelming impact his decisions may have on others.

This is what managerial responsibility in government is all about: it is the duty to achieve program goals, yes; but also the duty to do this in a way that comports with the basic tenets of a free society. Most of the checks on a bureaucracy are necessary to insure a responsive and a responsible bureaucracy.

Special Emphases in Employment

The public service of any jurisdiction is the property of the people who live, vote, and pay taxes in that jurisdiction. Understandably they feel they can use it to serve a number of purposes (beyond its original program operations) that are derived from its very existence. Thus, government personnel policy is sometimes affected by desires to attain social or economic ends that are not strictly within the bounds of sound administrative practice. Sometimes these ends can be served without violence to good management, sometimes not; nevertheless, all of them, must be faithfully adhered to as long as they are public policy.

Veteran Preference

The oldest such modification of managerial practice is the special preference in employment given by almost all jurisdictions in the United States to veterans of military service and often their wives or widows. For the most part, veteran preference has not seriously compromised the merit system. Requiring that veterans compete, limiting their advantage to a few rating points on an examination, confining preference to limited periods after discharge, excluding any preference once they are in the service—these are examples of preference provisions which keep merit principles relatively intact. The price thus paid in any adulteration of merit hiring has been small in view of the worthy aim of facilitating the return of veterans to civilian pursuits by having the government as employer take the lead and set the example.

The real problem emanates from the prostitution that takes place in almost all granting of special privilege: the tendency to view the privilege as a right, a disposition to supplement the privilege repeatedly with new benefits, a clamoring by other groups for equal privileges, an inclination to reduce eligibility requirements to qualify for the privilege, and a persistent temptation toward demagoguery on the part of petty politicians seeking favor with the privileged groups.

The most reprehensible features of veteran preference that have evolved from such tendencies are these:

1. Granting preference to "peace-time veterans" who never served in combat or even in time of war.
2. Granting preference to career military men who were never drafted, who had good careers in the

military by their own choice, and who enjoy retirement annuities therefrom.

3. Continuing preference in perpetuity, regardless of how long a man has been out of military service.
4. Extending preference to cover advancement and retention in the civil service, thereby reducing the incentive to perform at one's best and to earn promotion or retention.

In those jurisdictions that have such preference policies in effect, government managers should carefully assess their impact on effective performance; and wherever there is an adverse effect, they should have the courage to urge modification or repeal. There is often a lot of flag-waving chauvinism in behalf of the cause of veteran preference. True patriotism is more likely to be demonstrated by a genuine concern for the effectiveness of public services—and therefore the viability of democratic government.

Other Manpower Objectives

The more obvious it becomes that government is one of the major (if not the major) employer in every community, the more often it is turned to in times of public preoccupation with general unemployment. It is the first source thought of for jobs for the needy or the unemployed.

In an earlier chapter we pointed out how the public service can accommodate to such conditions by organizing its jobs so that they make maximum use of low-skilled personnel and minimum drain on scarcer, more expensive high-skilled talent; and by making sure that entry requirements are geared to actual job needs and not to preconceived notions engineered by protective occupational fraternities. If every governmental entity undertook a conscientious effort to achieve these goals, it would go far to relieve labor market problems in general; the chances are it would result in government doing more than its fair share in comparison with private employers.

But there are limits to what can be done to create legitimate work opportunities in public agencies. Some segments of the American public are too prone to think of government as a kind of gigantic eleemosynary institution so far as employment is concerned. Enthusiastic but inexperienced reformers are sometimes insistent that the public service be the prime source for training and hiring the unemployed and that it provide jobs regardless of its needs. Some even contend that actual preference be given to the least qualified—an outright reverse of merit.

When misguided efforts go this far, government managers must resist in the name of preservation of effective public services. Their stance is most persuasive when they have taken every possible step to insure that operation of the personnel system is geared realistically to the labor market; that it works without favor to preferred groups and without artificially-created barriers; and that its rewards are governed completely by demonstrated performance or capacity to perform.

The surest protection of competent governmental operations is relentless pursuit of true merit in every aspect of the personnel process. True merit *is*, after all, "equal opportunity"; it *is* "giving a chance to those who never had one." But it is not true merit to weaken the quality of the American public service.

The Tone of Administration

Several other considerations deserve emphasis in this discussion of the policy environment of the government manager with reference to personnel matters. No effort is made to cover every conceivable aspect of the subject. However, the points mentioned, though diverse among themselves, are illustrative of the action and behavior that influence the tone of administration.

Dealing With the Activist

A relatively new phenomenon in governmental circles is the behavior of the socially-minded civil servant who is more outspoken than before about problems of the day, some of which are subjects that his agency is enjoined to deal with, and who brings his extra-curricular interests into intimate juxtaposition with his daily duties. He may promote rallies of fellow civil servants to support such causes as peace, relief of poverty, or other worthy ends or to foster specific legislative or executive actions to further such causes. He may decorate his office or building corridors with posters or other abracadabra displaying his beliefs and concerns. He may seek publicity in newspapers or other media for his interests. He may dress unconventionally to draw attention to his disrespect for conventional mores. All these actions may be carried on while he presumably is faithfully and competently discharging the duties of his office.

Of course, there are some imperatives that warrant positive emphasis, regardless of how one might feel about the "doings" of any specific activist:

1. A civil servant is not deprived of his freedom of expression by virtue of being a government employee.
2. What a civil servant does *off* the job with respect to political causes or movements should be of no concern to management unless it compromises his effectiveness *on* the job.
3. What he does *on or off* the job should be given the benefit of the doubt except where it is clearly in violation of the law.

149

4. Management should encourage freedom of dissent; it should deliberately seek out the views of its staff, including those who obviously have some particular views to express; and it should make a conscious effort to enlist the enthusiasm and motivation of staff members who show a disposition to achieve worthy ends when these are within the scope of authority of the agency.

Having said this—and acknowledging that such policies religiously followed should substantially reduce potentiality for conflict—we must still consider the situation in which the activist, not management, is unreasonable and irresponsible. Just because his cause seems superficially above reproach and his concern sincere, it does not follow that he is free to do anything he pleases about it nor that all his colleagues or citizen clients will perceive his case as he does. He should enjoy the right of any citizen to have and to express opinions; but as a public servant he is not free to take advantage of his exposed position nor to compromise his sworn duties in order to advance his views.

There are some rough guidelines that public managers might follow in judging how to respond to unconventional employee behavior with respect to current issues of the day:

1. The foremost consideration is the job to be done. Any activity that takes an incumbent away from his job for longer periods than efficient performance can tolerate, that encroaches on his duty hours without charge to his personal leave, or that in any other way inhibits the prompt and effective performance of his duties, must be proscribed.
2. The very existence of an organization presumes a cohesive effort in support of its mission. While internal disagreement is inescapable and participative management should be a cardinal practice, once

decisions on controversial policies or procedures are finally made, it is the duty of all employees to work honestly to give them effect. The employee who refuses to do so is unequivocally insubordinate. A difference in judgment is not a defensible basis for defiance of administrative decision. To conclude otherwise would be to destroy the effectiveness, if not the existence, of an organization.

3. As stated before, only the most extraordinary and despicable circumstances can justify employee defiance of an administrative order: clear-cut evidence that the action or policy ordered is so patently illegal, corrupt, or unethical that men on both sides of a policy issue would readily acknowledge the fact. Under such circumstances, the level of management responsible for the action should be eliminated, not the defiant employee. This is by no means the same thing as simple disagreement over policy or procedure.

4. A public agency is created for a defined purpose, and it is often designed to serve a particular clientele. When an employee behaves in such a manner that this purpose or clientele is placed in jeopardy, such behavior must be forbidden. Minor protests by a few members of the clientele group are not necessarily indicative of such jeopardy; but extensive protest, resistance, or suffering by the clientele should be cause for prohibiting the employee's action or for dismissing him.

To some activists these criteria for managerial reaction may seem too harsh. To some managers they may seem too lenient. The proof will be in the implementation. The subject is too novel and unstructured to permit of complete and certain definition; more experience is necessary to reach that stage. The ideas offered here are in the nature of an interim policy until further study can lead to modification, addition, or refinement.

The Public "Right to Know"

At several points we have referred to the gold-fish-bowl character of the public administrator's life; and his actions in the area of personnel administration are no exception to this rule.

He owes it to the individual employees involved not to discuss contemplated actions with respect to promotions, separations, disciplinary measures, and the like outside the official family. But once decisions are made and the individuals affected have been duly informed, there should no longer be any secret about the actions. Premature "leaking" of prospective lay-offs, dismissals, or promotions—in spite of the relish of some newspapermen for such tidbits (on the theory that the reading public is eager for gossip)—serves no sound public or administrative purpose and is a disservice and embarrassment to the employees affected. As we have indicated before, the persons involved are entitled to be first "in the know"; from then on, the subject is public property.

This protection of the personal and private character of many relationships between management and the worker is the only exception to the standard personnel practice of open covenants, openly arrived at. Personnel policy is a proper matter of public interest. Where citizen groups (such as civil service leagues or professional associations) have a legitimate concern, they as well as employee groups are entitled to be informed of contemplated changes and to be heard regarding them if they should so desire. Many a personnel policy has a potential, or possibly only an imagined, impact on the customer—the citizen served by the agency involved. In any case, he has a right to know what is going on.

This consideration is not unlike that concerning the government manager's substantive program. The experienced executive should have no trouble in complying with it.

Ethics—Setting the Example

No more difficult, and sometimes agonizing, decision faces the public program manager than one that pits his personal welfare against his public duty: that is, the ethics of his action. Space does not permit a discussion of the underlying philosophy that should govern official behavior in a democracy. Thoughtful and useful treatments of that subject may be found in a number of other works, several of which are cited in the bibliography at the end of this volume. Suffice it to emphasize here only a few of the most elementary precepts of ethical performance in the public service:

- The public interest must always, and without equivocation, be placed ahead of private interest or personal gain.
- Efforts to corrupt must uncompromisingly be ferreted out and exposed.
- The interests of those not immediately pressing their case before the public official must be taken into account along with those of protagonists who are.
- High ethical standards must be demanded of all employees in the service.
- Employees must be helped to appreciate what these standards are and what is expected of them as workers in conforming.
- The public interest must be placed above the interest of employees as a group as well as above that of any individual employee.

Clearly these precepts impose obligations on officials in the way of leadership in formulating objectives and codes of practice, in training employees to understand and adhere to such criteria, and in setting examples by their

153

own behavior. Establishing the guidelines and processes by which they will be judged provides another excellent occasion for enlisting the thoughtful participation of affected employees.

Ethics embrace considerably more than right conduct with respect to financial interests or the acceptance of bribes and favors. The more subtle applications relate to program and policy content. They require taking into account all factors and facts relating to a subject or project before conclusions are drawn. They mean discounting personal opinions until all the evidence is in. They entail a dispassionate and detached approach to all big or little policy and case decisions that public employees are called upon to make.

Such ethical considerations relate back to the subject of employee activism, to the importance of maintaining a worker's (particularly a professional's) integrity and his obligation to render even-handed, impartial administration. An employee's action that creates an adverse reflection on such integrity or impartiality cannot be condoned. On the other hand, to expect him to violate the fundamental ethical obligations of his own profession is in itself unethical.

Perhaps the most important single factor in issues of ethical conduct in the public service is the influence of executive example. Employees have a persistent way of discerning the attitudes, to say nothing of the behavior, of their administrative leaders when it comes to morality. What the supervisor does or says has a potent effect on the subordinate, no matter how independent-minded the subordinate is. In all matters of ethical performance the most unambiguous standard, the most effective training, and the most assured enforcement derive from the high principles, uncompromising integrity, and irreproachable conduct of the government manager at every level of the service.

9

Working With the Personnel Specialists

A<small>T MANY POINTS</small> in this book we have stressed that personnel administration is a shared responsibility: employees have their roles, and on the management side the program manager and the personnel specialist are jointly responsible. However, little has been said about the last group—those who spend full time on matters of personnel policy and management. We have been deliberately vague about this area so that concentrated attention could be given to the subject in the present chapter. The references to the "personnel office" and the "personnel man" in preceding chapters were purposely generic; they should be taken to mean collectively those organizations and persons who are charged with full-time attention to employing, motivating, paying, and dealing with public employees.

Personnel Organization

Nor have we made a clear distinction between central

155

personnel agencies and departmental personnel offices. The former are usually established by law, entail some degree of identification with the chief executive of a jurisdiction or over-all executive management, and are located in the hierarchy above the level of the department head and other government managers. On the other hand, the typical personnel office is usually an integral part of an operating department or establishment, with general responsibility to the agency head but with a strong functional responsibility, in view of its specialization, to the central personnel agency.

The Central Personnel Authority

A central personnel agency may be headed by a multi-membered personnel board or civil service commission, usually with an executive head reporting to such body; or by a single personnel executive reporting to the chief executive of the jurisdiction. In the latter case, the typical form of organization includes a commission or board working in an advisory or policy-making capacity with the personnel executive. A personnel office in an operating department, on the other hand, is almost invariably headed by a single personnel administrator reporting to the head or assistant head of the department.

Much discussion appears in the literature over the issue of the so-called "independence" of central personnel agencies. This was originally a concern of the civil service reformers who were preoccupied with keeping political heads of government from succumbing to spoils politics. Accordingly, bi-partisan bodies ostensibly independent of the chief executive were made the *sine qua non* apparatus of merit systems—in order, it was theorized, to prevent patronage-seeking politicians from interfering. More recently, with the merit idea more firmly entrenched and most governmental units seeking candidates instead of fending off party hacks seeking jobs, central personnel agencies have been drawn closer into the chief executive orbit. The creation of state, county, and municipal personnel directorships—responsible to governors or to county or city managers—is one evidence of this trend.

The Manager's Interests

In any event, the question of the independence of personnel agencies from chief executives has little impact on government managers from department heads on down. The chief executive of a jurisdiction may well feel the need for some direct involvement in personnel policy development and implementation, of which he may be deprived by existence of the classical personnel agency that has no responsibility to him. On the other hand, from the vantage point of a department head or his subordinates, it does not make much difference whether the central personnel establishment is an instrument of the chief executive, or an independent entity, or something in between. In any case, such an office has government-wide authority and is located at a more central and higher level —with greater finality of decision.

For those executives in departments large enough to possess their own personnel offices, the locus of personnel expertise and leadership is in those offices. There may be some direct contacts between operators and the central personnel agency, but most contacts will be through the department's own personnel office.

Such a wide range of conditions exists—with obvious contrasts as between large cities and major states on the one hand and small jurisdictions on the other—it is difficult to generalize about relationships. But in effect, there are two basic kinds of relationships between operating officials and personnel specialists: (1) those where the operator is dealing with a personnel organization subordinate and responsible to him; and (2) those where he is dealing with a personnel organization that is responsible to his chief or someone above that level. In the latter situation, the operating official has only the power of persuasion in influencing personnel matters, whereas in the first situation the manager himself is responsible for the operation of a personnel office. The principal thrust of the comment in this chapter is to be on the situation in which he has the greater authority, where he is in effect—with technical advice and help, of course—the top personnel director as well as operating head of his agency. At the same time, much of the philosophy expressed is pointedly applicable to the second situation, especially those observations that pertain to sharing in the over-all personnel function, to the joint responsibility of manager and personnel expert.

Making Use of the Personnel Office

A personnel office will be about as good as the general manager in charge expects it to be. If he looks upon it as a routine operation and staffs it accordingly, it will undoubtedly be a very pedestrian activity. It will seldom initiate, it will cloak itself comfortably with the "rules", and it will almost certainly be behind the times.

But if the manager expects his personnel office to be a live-wire organization, if he wants it to exert some imagination while still adhering to high-principled conduct, and if he intends for it to have some positive impact on the agency's manpower situation, then he will do well to follow some simple elements of administrative doctrine:

1. He will ask the personnel office to be his eyes and ears on all matters relating to "people problems" throughout the organization. He will expect the specialists to be close to operations, to know what

is going on, to have the confidence of supervisors and workers alike, and to report to him any existing or prospective difficulties they diagnose, along with suggested remedies.

2. He will bring the personnel office into the inner councils of his top executive family. He will:
   - keep the office informed of any thinking or plans that might conceivably affect or be affected by personnel considerations (and there are few prospects that are not so related).
   - have the chief or top representatives of the personnel office present in all top-level staff meetings, where they can participate freely and openly in all administrative discussion and planning.
   - consult frequently and encourage his subordinate managers to consult with the key personnel specialists, not only to solicit their views but to exchange opinions and discuss management issues in a spirit of mutual counsel.

3. He will urge and equip the personnel office to plan ahead, to anticipate recruitment problems, to keep up with the effects of the outside labor market and salaries, and to probe what employees are thinking so that their attitudes and reactions may be anticipated. (Note that verb "equip"; unless a personnel office is adequately staffed it cannot carry on such farsighted functions.)

4. He will insist that the personnel officer and his aides contribute significantly to answering the really difficult questions: how jobs might be restructured to respond to the labor market and better serve the organization; what new sources for recruitment might be tapped; how poor workers might be better adjusted; what the real training needs are and how they might best be met; where economies can

be realized in the personnel program; what the actual impact of incentive awards is; how thorny conflicts between management and worker can best be resolved; in what respects qualification standards deserve overhauling; how the evaluation of performance might be improved; and so on.

5. He will see to it that the personnel office embraces the full range of functions that have a bearing on the acquisition, development, and motivation of employees—not only the traditional chores of employment, classification, and enforcement of policy, but also training, health and safety, negotiation with unions, counseling, and research, including attitude surveys. In this connection, he will see to it that the personnel officer and his staff are exposed to what is going on elsewhere, that they attend and participate in professional meetings, and that they themselves take part in administrative training that will help them adjust to the times and perform effectively.

6. He will make it clear that his personnel officer is there to represent him—to subordinates, outside interest groups, and the press—on all matters relating to personnel policy or procedure. He will give the personnel officer sufficient authority and back him up with sufficient force to command the respect of all these groups.

7. He will make the role of the personnel office clear to his subordinate managers—emphasizing its services and expertise, clarifying in what respects it must act as a control agent (on such matters as appointment processing and position classification), specifying its delegated authority to act for him, and indicating circumstances and formats for resolving any disagreements between operators and personnel specialists.

8. He will staff the personnel office in such quantity

and quality that it can in reality perform in the fashion that he demands. (This aspect of the subject deserves separate, more detailed comment later in this chapter.)

Expecting the impossible? Perhaps, and in some circumstances almost certainly so. But the government executive who believes in the philosophy enunciated above, who tries genuinely to handle his personnel operation and deal with his personnel staff in the manner outlined, is going to have a more successful personnel program and fewer personnel problems than the executive who treats these matters disdainfully—or, worse still, ignores them.

The Personnel Manager and Specialist

What, then, must the person in charge of the personnel operation and his staff be like? How can their expertise be insured, along with their understanding and appreciation of the general goals and problems of the government agency of which they are a part? Here, again, we run the risk of over-idealization, of prescribing the unattainable. However, this author is firmly of the opinion that public administration can never live up to all that is expected of it in the decades ahead unless we live by the poet's code that *"a man's reach should exceed his grasp."*

The "Complete" Personnel Man

What He Needs to Know. To be a specialist in manpower matters means much more than knowledge of technique. It is taken for granted that the personnel man or woman must be familiar with occupations, examining procedures, job analysis, educational methods, and other such technical matters. What is often overlooked is that

161

he needs to be more than a technician if he is truly to serve modern public administration. For example:

1. He needs to be broad-gauged enough to understand and feel some empathy with efforts to solve the great issues facing our society: the population explosion, pollution, conservation, urban blight, racial tension, poverty, transportation, education, automation, international conflict, and all the others. He must be the focal point for instilling an appreciation of the magnitude of—and the competing prescriptions for dealing with—these problems among all persons related to the public service, from potential recruits to long-time staff members.

2. He must also appreciate and be prepared to act on the reality that the nature and organization of work, taken together, is the great motivator. He must be ready to design and propose personnel measures that build on this fundamental truth, along with recognizing the importance of public functions in coping with the great problems.

3. He needs a deep understanding of employment sociology—of the changes that are taking place all around us: the civil rights revolution; the needs of groups heretofore disadvantaged or discriminated against, not only racial minorities, but also women, older workers, the handicapped, and so forth; and the special problems of labor organization in government service.

4. He requires sufficient grasp of the nature and significance of behavioral research that is current so that he can appraise its quality and its practitioners, so that he knows where to turn for help. Every personnel manager cannot be his own scientist, but he can know enough to make use of sound researchers and theorists in the field.

5. With the fantastic growth of state and city govern-

ments in the United States and its parallel in other countries, he must be mindful of the possibilities and fruitfulness of intergovernmental cooperation. Mutual assistance or joint action is called for on a number of fronts: consolidation of recruitment and examination procedures, standardization in pay and retirement systems, and mobility of key personnel, to name only a few. No fully-prepared public personnel executive can isolate himself from such opportunities for collaborative endeavors among different jurisdictions.

6. Not to downgrade technique entirely, it should be added that there are many new technical developments with which the progressive personnel specialist must keep abreast: the use of statistics, computers, manpower forecasting and planning, and other quantitative methods; constructive job engineering and redesign; testing for creativity and for motivation; sophisticated training experiences; and various others.

Perhaps the paragon who knows all these things equally well does not exist, but this should not stop the government manager from holding these requisites as his goal in seeking and developing a personnel staff.

How He Needs to Behave. On top of all this fund of information and understanding, the personnel specialist needs the talent, personality, and character to play several very sensitive roles:

1. He requires the capacity to serve as an *advisor*. To be sought, his insight and counsel has to be mature and wise.
2. He must be an *interpreter*—a broker between supervisor and employee, between rule and situation, and between policy intent and operating need.
3. He cannot escape being a *controller*. The sheer vol-

163

ume of work necessitates delegation of some "yes or no" line authority to him.

4. He needs to be a *diagnostician.* He must have the talent to sense what is really behind a condition or attitude, and perhaps more importantly, to know how to go about getting the unvarnished facts.

5. He must set an *example.* Operating managers have a right to expect their personnel experts not only to *talk* but to *show* the way—to practice what they preach, to be first-rate supervisors, to put all personnel policies and ideals into effect in their own shops, to exploit every means for economy, to run model organizations.

It may be difficult to find all these capacities or qualities in any one person; but again, what is not ready-made can be developed. The important thing is to have such a prescription as a yardstick. Many able people are capable of attaining these standards—especially if the personnel profession is allowed to build up a reservoir of outstanding talent in the first place.

Filling Personnel Jobs

If anything approximating the ideal for the personnel staff is to be realized, it is obvious that the practice of using the personnel office as the dumping ground for mediocrity cannot be tolerated. Not that most personnel offices in government today are staffed *primarily* with mediocre talent; it is simply a fact that too many operating managers have regarded the personnel function so inadequately or unimaginatively that they have foisted off on to it too many misfits and ne'er-do-wells—on the theory that almost anyone ought to be able to do a personnel job.

The result is that too many personnel offices struggle along with far more than their fair share of the organization's cast-offs. Even when the top people in the personnel office are of high caliber, they cannot function in the manner envisaged in this chapter with millstones of incompetence hanging about their necks. It is not enough to say that personnel directors should have the courage to get rid of such weak links in the personnel management chain, when these links were forged elsewhere and expressly installed in the personnel organization by an unwitting operating management.

The whole matter comes down to the degree of understanding and appreciation for the personnel function that government managers—up and down the line—possess. If they look upon it as contemplated in this book, they will have no trouble in attracting and holding a talented, highly-motivated personnel staff. A few pointers to facilitate this process are in order before we close.

What to Avoid

First and foremost, it should be obvious that personnel work is not to be entrusted to those with only clerical experience or a clerical outlook. To perform professionally requires professional training; furthermore, it requires a broad educational background encompassing good insight into the world's problems and the world's work. Fulfilling the expectations of top management calls for capacities and education that may be acquired in a variety of ways, but rarely can these be achieved with only a secondary school preparation. Indeed, graduate study beyond the baccalaureate degree is coming more and more to be the norm for full-fledged personnel jobs.

As for personal aptitudes, it is not enough to determine that a candidate "likes people" and has a pleasing, easy-going personality. A well-adjusted person he must certainly be, but he can seldom get by simply with a kind of happy rapport with other human beings. Sometimes this sort of personality is utterly unable to summon the courage to make the difficult decisions that personnel administration so often requires.

Where to Look

With these precautions out of the way, where can the operating manager turn to find his personnel staff? In the absence of adequate local sources, he must make a region-wide or even a nation-wide search. Only the largest metropolitan areas are likely to have a substantial reservoir of local talent. Assistance from professional personnel organizations may often be secured to develop recruitment possibilities.

Within a jurisdiction, several approaches are available. The possibility of using junior personnel jobs as training assignments for a variety of other managerial or even technical workers should not be overlooked. Following some formal in-service training courses, even specialists in other disciplines may be used successfully in personnel offices. After several years of such experience they may again return to their first field. Rotation of engineers, accountants, police officers, social workers, foresters, revenue agents, and many others through personnel assignments has often been useful in building supervisory and executive capacity.

At the senior levels it is sometimes practicable to place persons who have had a combination of such experiences in key personnel jobs. Some of the best-run government agencies have made it a practice to fill their personnel directorships with people who have had operating experience. The benefits both for operating management and for personnel policy and practice are frequently striking.

The sum and substance of the point made here is that there is no royal single road to finding able staff for personnel jobs. Certainly, of all occupations, personnel specialists should not fall into the error made in so many other fields—restrictions on entry that are too arbitrary and rigid to serve the highest purposes of the profession or to accommodate to changing circumstances.

Developing Capacity

The personnel staff should not be "cobbler's children" when it comes to in-service training or taking advantage of outside professional study. With training and self-renewal having become major necessities of modern administration, personnel workers—above all—should have these experiences themselves. As previously indicated, growth on the job can be achieved not only by participation in formal course work but also by attendance and involvement in outside professional meetings and activities. It is incumbent upon general operating managers to insist that their personnel specialists get as much of this exposure as possible.

In addition, it is well to see that members of the personnel staff, particularly the key people, get practical experience outside their own offices. Like workers in any other field, a personnel man who stays too long in the same spot is bound to grow stale. One of the best ways to get new perspectives and a fresh appreciation of the old job is an exchange assignment with another jurisdiction, an operating responsibility, or even a foreign consultantship.

In short, to secure a top-notch personnel staff, government management has to pay for it—in a broad conception of what the staff should be like, of how it should be recruited and utilized, and of how it should be trained and developed.

A Concluding Word

A discussion of working with personnel specialists

should not conclude without emphasis on a most basic consideration: the vital role of research. The mistake often made in reference to personnel research is to assume that the results of studies in other places are equally applicable to one's own establishment. Much may be transferrable, certainly enough to warrant having personnel staff keep abreast of systematic research elsewhere. This may be especially true of studies of organization for personnel work, basic behavioral phenomena, the effects of veteran preference, comparisons among career systems, the benefits of mobility, and other such universal issues.

However, too great reliance on the utility of other people's research overlooks three factors:

1. The social sciences, and particularly the study of human behavior and motivation, are not well enough developed that they may be relied on without constant rechecking as conditions change.
2. There are always conditions in each locality and each major organization that are peculiar to them, thus requiring tailor-made studies of effects or alternatives suitable only to the locale.
3. The techniques and findings of research evolve, making it essential that yesterday's approach be updated continually as new evidence is produced.

Hence, it is imperative that every major governmental organization have the capacity to conduct a modest amount of personnel research attuned to its particular needs. Examples of subjects and issues that call primarily for study on the local scene are: the optimum (as distinguished from presumed) qualifications needed to perform various classes of work; the kind of working environment that equates with the highest productivity; the impact of alternative modes of organizing tasks into jobs; the effects on performance of specific training programs; the results of different degrees of delegation of authority; comparisons of pay, retirement, leave, and other benefits with those of other jurisdictions; attitude surveys relating both to personnel conditions and to feelings about work objectives or methods; analyses of different styles of supervision as related to the kind of work, for example contrasting police, teaching, or public health services; and numerous others that will come to the mind of every thoughtful manager as they apply to his own situation.

In addition to providing adequate in-house staff to be responsible for such studies, a public agency may call upon outside groups to augment its staff or make special studies beyond its competence. Many universities and other institutions are equipped to be useful in this regard; and they would welcome opportunities to apply their research know-how to government administration and to contribute to the solution of important policy issues.

This much stress is being placed on the subject of research, because it is the least developed and least exploited of the public personnel functions. This is less true of industrial personnel administration, and still less applicable to military personnel operations, but the civil services have lagged behind. The public administrator who wants to derive the most from having a specialized personnel staff will insist that one of its most important activities be a continuous program of research. Only in this way can he be sure that policies and procedures being formulated will be relevant to his agency's needs and will offer hope of dealing constructively with its personnel problems.

10

The Service Concept

A FTER READING the foregoing chapters, the practicing or embryo government manager may well ask: "If I do all the things suggested here, what time will I have for my substantive operations, my regular program work?" This is a good question, and it deserves an answer; but before attempting that answer one must ask still another question: "Under what conception of administration should the answer be formulated?"

Doing the Operating Job

If we think of the manager as the principal technician in his operation, it is difficult to come up with an acceptable answer to the first question. If he is to spend a great deal of his time second-guessing his subordinates—and often re-doing their work—he will be hard pressed for time to give adequate attention to personnel matters. On the other hand, if he views his job as mainly one of working through other people, everything he does under the banner of personnel management is actually part of his operating job. This, then, is the answer: to keep his operating responsibilities in order, the administrator must keep his personnel responsibilities in order. The one is almost indistinguishable from the other, for the bulk of his operating job is done through sound personnel management.

Such a view of his responsibilities is more appropriate in the case of a top-ranking executive than in the case of a lower-level supervisor. The higher up the hierarchy one goes the more personnel responsibilities one feels. At the lower end of the ladder, supervisors may well be more occupied with substantive decisions than with decisions about people; but even there they are either following—or ignoring—the precepts in this book whenever they instruct, correct, praise, support, or reverse an employee. At the top —while the process of weighing major substantive issues attracts the most outside attention—more of this analysis and judgment are institutional products than the public ordinarily realizes, with the participation of high-level executives being the least time-consuming stage in the chain of events. In the higher ranks much time is taken up with determining who shall do what, with what authority, and how well they do it, with what result.

Senior managers are primarily communicators and reactors—sending and receiving messages throughout the organization. In this process, they make many substantive judgments, but usually on the basis of facts and alternatives presented to them. Their stimulation of and response to the staff in this exchange is inseparable from their operating judgments. Thus, the more complete answer to the original question is this: it is an illusion to think of personnel decisions as occupying separate time from operating decisions. Personnel decisions have to do with *how* the operating decisions are made; they are inextricably bound up with operations. The administrator does not pause at cer-

172

tain times of the day and "do his personnel work;" he is doing it every time he assigns, informs, reacts to, or deals with people. Personnel work is the warp and woof of his everyday tasks.

Political and Career Executives

In this book we have not made a sharp distinction between political and career executives. Because of their far greater number and continuity, career managers are more likely to find the doctrine relevant than political heads. But the philosophy presented is equally applicable to the politically-appointed or elected chiefs as it is to the permanent staff. Its relevance has more to do with the concept of the job and the style of the official than with the method of his appointment. Of course, those who preoccupy themselves with their representational functions vis-a-vis outside clientele groups and leave direction of the staff to others will have less impact on personnel administration than those who take charge of matters of organization, utilization, indoctrination, and performance.

In reality, there are more similarities than differences in the roles and responsibilities of political and career government managers. Their successes and failures depend on many of the same qualities and attributes. Zeal for the public interest is just as necessary in the one case as it is in the other. In brief, the issue comes down to a common denominator when we think of their responsibility for service to society.

What is Service?

Basically, "service" in the public service means carrying out the law faithfully and impartially, and in this way serving the public interest. Of course, it is not all that

173

simple. Finding out what the public interest is constitutes problem number one. Building the organizational and personnel arrangements, perhaps involving hundreds or thousands of workers, is the second problem. Being faithful and impartial requires working at both every day and every moment.

At the same time, "service" means accomplishing something; and this entails factors of efficiency and human attitudes of enthusiasm and dedication. It is not enough to be upright and technically within the law. Effective government administration demands more than that. It demands human understanding and warmth. It requires zeal and concern for missions and goals. It therefore embraces getting the most done with available wherewithal, and it encompasses a determination to extend the service to broader clienteles and to wider purposes.

Public servants are often accused of "empire building." Newspapermen and out-of-office politicians see desires for expansion only as nefarious plots for power and prestige. There is another interpretation: government executives who strive to extend their services are the highly-motivated ones who cannot rest content to see problems unsolved or citizens' needs unmet. Often they are the very ones we should be holding up as examples to a new generation of civil servants. Chances are they have real concern for the effectiveness of their programs and have the personal attributes of aggressiveness and courage too often lacking among those on the public payroll.

No, public service implies neither bland neutrality nor supine obsequiousness. If it means anything, it means leadership—by career and political executive alike. But it also entails getting all we can out of what we have. A passion for economy, squeezing every value out of existing resources, is a quality wholly consistent with a service attitude; and it calls for imbuing the entire staff with the same determination.

The Service-Motivated Executive

Thus, a great deal of what we seek in the service-minded public executive—a zeal for the program mission, a yen to make it more effective, and a desire to stretch resources to the utmost—is dependent on his leadership inside and outside the government agency. This brand of leadership inspires a staff while at the same time it wins the plaudits of citizens and their representatives. As in the classic definition of sound public relations (that appeared some years ago in a Public Personnel Association pamphlet by Eleanor Ruhl Batson), it is "doing good and getting credit for it."

The requisites for executive behavior set forth in Chapter 1 are worth reemphasis in this connection. The ideal public executive is one who understands his role and his function in perspective, who has the inclination for personal growth and self-renewal, who is receptive to change, and who has a genuine concern for people. Those who display such attributes are most likely to be exemplars of the service motive.

We must leave to other publications a more refined spinning out of some of the theses set forth here. The essence of what we have to say about service to the public is simply this: the government manager must achieve the mission assigned to him through people. Their failure or success is his nemesis—or his glory. And he has much more to do with that performance than he is sometimes inclined to admit.

Presumably the political executive excels in talents for the external relationships with the general public and their representatives, while the career executive excels in the internal relationships—getting the job done through the staff. But, for completeness, each needs some of the interests and attributes of the other. The career manager needs to have some "fire in his belly" on behalf of the function he is working at; and the political manager needs to show some concern for and spend some time at organizing and motivating the staff. When each shares at least a measure of the zeal and skill of the other, they not only complement each other, they are more likely to understand each other. The combination is unbeatable.

Bibliography

The following list of readings is a very limited one, reflecting an effort to identify only the most significant books, and a few pamphlets and articles, that relate to government personnel administration. They are organized under headings that indicate their general content rather than by the chapters of this book. The first grouping is included to provide a "feel" for the administrative scene in American government and for some of the problems and challenges facing public executives.

Background Issues on Public Administration

Paul H. Appleby, *Big Democracy*. New York: Alfred A. Knopf, 1945.

Marshall E. Dimock, *Administrative Vitality*. New York: Harper & Row, 1959.

Marshall E. Dimock and Gladys O. Dimock, *Public Administration*. 4th Ed. New York: Holt, Rinehart and Winston, 1969.

John W. Gardner, *Excellence; Can We Be Equal and Excellent Too?* New York: Harper & Row, 1961.

John W. Gardner, *Self-Renewal: The Individual and the Innovative Society.* New York: Harper & Row, 1964.

Harold J. Laski, "The Limitations of the Expert." *Harper's Magazine,* December 1930.

Walter Lippmann, *The Public Philosophy.* Boston: Little, Brown and Co., 1955.

John D. Weaver, *The Great Experiment: An Intimate View of the Everyday Workings of the Federal Government.* Boston: Little, Brown and Co., 1965.

Philosophy and Problems of Government Personnel Administration

Robert T. Golembiewski and Michael Cohen, eds., *People in Public Service: A Reader in Public Personnel Administration.* Itasca, Ill.: F. E. Peacock Publishers, 1970.

George A. Graham, *Morality in American Politics.* New York: Random House, 1952.

W. Brooke Graves, *Federalism and Public Employment.* Washington: Federal Professional Association, 1965.

Donald Hayman and O. Glenn Stahl, *Political Activity Restrictions: An Analysis with Recommendations.* Personnel Report No. 636. Chicago: Public Personnel Association, 1963.

H. Eliot Kaplan, *The Law of Civil Service.* New York: Matthew Bender and Co., 1958.

Wayne A. R. Leys, *Ethics for Policy Decisions.* New York: Prentice-Hall, 1952.

Frederick C. Mosher, *Democracy and the Public Service.* New York: Oxford University Press, 1968.

O. Glenn Stahl, *Public Personnel Administration.* 6th Ed. New York: Harper & Row, 1971.

Telford Taylor, "The Ethics of Public Office." *The Saturday Evening Post,* April 16, 1960.

Paul P. Van Riper, *History of the United States Civil Service.* Evanston: Row, Peterson and Co., 1958.

Public Service Manpower

John J. Corson and R. Shale Paul, *Men Near the Top: Filling Key Posts in the Federal Service.* Supplementary Paper No. 20. Committee for Economic Development. Baltimore: The Johns Hopkins Press, 1966.

J. J. Donovan, ed., *Recruitment and Selection in the Public Service.* Chicago: Public Personnel Association, 1968.

Jacob W. Getzels and Philip W. Jackson, *Creativity and Intelligence.* New York: John Wiley & Sons, 1962.

Department of Health, Education, and Welfare; Office of State Merit Systems, *An Equal Opportunity Program for State and Local Government Employment.* Washington, 1970.

Milton M. Mandell, *The Selection Process: Choosing the Right Man for the Job.* New York: American Management Association, 1964.

Municipal Manpower Commission, *Governmental Manpower for Tomorrow's Cities.* New York: McGraw-Hill Book Co., 1962.

National Manpower Council, *Government and Manpower.* New York: Columbia University Press, 1964.

David T. Stanley, *The Higher Civil Service: An Evaluation of Federal Personnel Practices.* Washington: The Brookings Institution, 1964.

W. Lloyd Warner, "The Careers of American Business and Government Executives: A Comparative Analysis." In George B. Strother, ed., *Social Science Approaches to Business Behavior.* Homewood, Ill.: Richard D. Irwin and the Dorsey Press, 1962.

The Job Structure

Ismar Baruch, ed., *Position Classification in the Public Service.* Chicago: Public Personnel Association, 1941 (reprinted in 1965).

Robert N. Ford, *Motivation Through the Work Itself.* New York: American Management Association, 1969.

U. S. Civil Service Commission, *Classification Principles and Policies.* Personnel Management Series No. 16. Washington, 1963.

Kenneth O. Warner and J. J. Donovan, eds., *Practical Guidelines to Public Pay Administration.* Vol. 1, 1963; Vol. 2, 1965. Chicago: Public Personnel Association.

Motivation, Development, and Performance

Kenneth T. Byers, ed., *Employee Training and Development in the Public Service.* Chicago: Public Personnel Association, 1970.

Saul W. Gellerman, *Management by Motivation.* New York: American Management Association, 1968.

Raymond Krah, *Administrative Control of Sick Leave.* Personnel Report No. 544. Chicago: Public Personnel Association, 1955.

Harold J. Leavitt, *Managerial Psychology.* 2nd Ed. Chicago: University of Chicago Press, 1964.

Rensis Likert, *New Patterns of Management.* New York: McGraw-Hill Book Co., 1961.

Rensis Likert, *The Human Organization: Its Management and Value.* New York: McGraw-Hill Book Co., 1967.

Felix M. Lopez, Jr., *Evaluating Employee Performance.*

Chicago: Public Personnel Association, 1968.

Ernest J. McCormick, *Human Factors Engineering*. 2nd Ed. New York: McGraw-Hill Book Co., 1964.

Douglas McGregor, *The Human Side of Enterprise*. New York: McGraw-Hill Book Co., 1960.

John M. Pfiffner and Marshall Fels, *The Supervision of Personnel: Human Relations in the Management of Men*. 3rd Ed. Englewood Cliffs, N.J.: Prentice-Hall, 1964.

Lowell S. Trowbridge, *Human Relations*. Waterford, Conn.: National Foremen's Institute, 1968.

Unions in the Public Service

Advisory Commission on Intergovernmental Relations, *Labor-Management Policies for State and Local Government*. Washington, 1969.

Felix A. Nigro, *Management-Employee Relations in the Public Service*. Chicago: Public Personnel Association, 1969.

A. H. Raskin, "Collective Bargaining and the Public Interest." In *Challenges To Collective Bargaining*. Edited by Lloyd Ulman. Papers prepared for the Thirtieth American Assembly, Columbia University. Englewood Cliffs, N.J.: Prentice-Hall, 1967.

Carmen D. Saso, *Coping With Public Employee Strikes*. Chicago: Public Personnel Association, 1970.

Jack Stieber, "Collective Bargaining in the Public Sector." In *Challenges to Collective Bargaining*. Edited by Lloyd Ulman. Papers prepared for the Thirtieth American Assembly, Columbia University. Englewood Cliffs, N.J.: Prentice-Hall, 1967.

Twentieth Century Fund, *Pickets at City Hall*. Report and Recommendations of the Twentieth Century Fund Task Force on Labor Disputes in Public Employment. New York, 1970.

181

Kenneth O. Warner, ed., *Management Relations with Organized Public Employees.* Chicago: Public Personnel Association, 1963.

Kenneth O. Warner and Mary L. Hennessy, *Public Management at the Bargaining Table.* Chicago: Public Personnel Association, 1967.

Organization for Personnel Administration

Sydney D. Bailey, *The Secretariat of the United Nations.* United Nations Study No. 11. New York: Carnegie Endowment for International Peace, 1962.

Cecil E. Goode, *Personnel Research Frontiers: A Review of Personnel Research Activities and Facilities, with Special Reference to their Implications for Government.* Chicago: Public Personnel Association, 1958.

Dag Hammarskjold, *The International Civil Servant in Law and in Fact.* A Lecture Delivered to Congregation. Oxford: Clarendon Press, 1961.

Donald R. Harvey, *The Civil Service Commission.* New York: Praeger Publishers, 1970.

Georges Langrod, *The International Civil Service: Its Origins, Its Nature, Its Evolution.* Dobbs Ferry, N.Y.: Oceana Publications, 1963.

Tom Page, ed., *The Public Personnel Agency and the Chief Executive: A Symposium,* Personnel Report No. 601. Chicago: Public Personnel Association, 1960.

Wallace S. Sayre and Frederick C. Mosher, *An Agenda for Research in Public Personnel Administration.* Washington: National Planning Association, 1959.

O. Glenn Stahl, "Tomorrow's Generation of Personnel Managers." In *Public Personnel Administration— Progress and Prospects.* Personnel Report No. 681 (including a commentary by Edward C. Gallas). Chicago: Public Personnel Association, 1968.

Index

183